The Facilitative Leader

The Facilitative Leader

Managing Performance Without Controlling People

Steve Reilly

BEP BUSINESS EXPERT PRESS

First published in 2017 by
Business Expert Press, LLC
222 East 46th Street, New York, NY 10017
www.businessexpertpress.com

ISBN-13: 978-1-63157-625-6 (paperback)
ISBN-13: 978-1-63157-626-3 (e-book)

Business Expert Press Human Resource Management and Organizational Behavior Collection

Collection ISSN: 1946-5637 (print)
Collection ISSN: 1946-5645 (electronic)

Cover and interior design by S4Carlisle Publishing Services
Private Ltd., Chennai, India

First edition: 2017

10 9 8 7 6 5 4 3 2 1

Printed in the United States of America.

Dedication

To my most treasured, Maddy and Alexis

Abstract

This book is for anyone who has either worked for or been a difficult boss. It will especially benefit those new to management and struggling to figure out how to lead a team without being too controlling. Using the foundational ideas of clear expectations, honest and constructive feedback, and personal accountability, it is possible to manage people's performance without controlling their behaviors. It is a shift in priorities and mind set, but has been proven with such companies like Nike, Microsoft, Caterpillar, Cisco Systems, United Healthcare, and many other Fortune 100 companies.

Keywords

accountability, coaching, empowerment, expectations, facilitating, feedback, leadership, management, performance.

Contents

Acknowledgment

I learned most of my management skills by mistake. At least in the American Business community, being promoted to a people management position is often like the first time you take an infant home from a hospital—there is no manual on how to ensure you make it through the first nine months. This was exactly my experience when I moved into my first people management role. Although it was an excellent learning experience, I improved my leadership skills at the expense of my team members. I stumbled into situations, sometimes difficult situations with difficult employees, and exited often wiser if not also humbler. So I dedicate this to the people I managed both effectively and less than effectively over the years, in hopes that other new managers can avoid replicating my mistakes.

Control or Engage?

The best example of leadership in our culture is the one most often ignored; good parenting.

—Peter Senge, The Fifth Discipline

EVERY SUMMER since she was born, my daughter Alexis and I have traveled from our home in Seattle to Cape May, a resort town on the southern coast of New Jersey. My parents and nine brothers and sisters rent as many charming Victorian houses as are required to hold all the children, grandchildren, wives, husbands, and significant others for a week-long family reunion. To a worrying father, each new stage in his child's life holds its own peculiar terrors. This was Alex's fifth year at the New Jersey shore, so she no longer wanted Dad looking over her shoulder, especially at the beach. I knew my job however: to catalog the smorgasbord of dangers available to my daughter and to prevent her from sampling any of them—especially drowning. As a child, I had spent each summer at the shore with my own family, so I knew them all: rip tides, under-tows, waves too big to handle, and so on. Alex had grown up on Puget Sound, where the water is too bone-chillingly cold to entice a toddler into trouble. Standing in front of our beach blanket on the first day, surveying our stretch of beach, I called Alexis over. She looked up at me with her blue-gray eyes as if to say, "What now, Dad?" "Alex, let me tell you what the rules are, OK?" "OK," she replied. "When you are in the water you have to stay in front of the lifeguard stand." She agreed.

"And see those ropes?" I said, pointing. "Don't go near them, because you might get tangled up." "Okay," she said again. "Oh, and one more thing." "What?" she said, rolling her eyes. "It doesn't matter how shallow the water is before the wave comes. It matters how deep it is after the wave breaks. It shouldn't be any deeper than the middle of your chest." I used my hand to show her where the middle of her chest was. "That's all. Have fun and don't throw sand at your cousins." Then Alex ran into the water to ride the waves and I opened my beach chair and sat down at the water's edge to read *The Philadelphia Inquirer*. Occasionally I folded down the corner of my paper to check on her.

Just as I began to dive into the editorial page, one of my sisters put her beach chair next to me along the water's edge. As we see each other usually just once a year, this was a good time to fill in the blanks on each other's lives and parenting challenges. My sister has a number of children, and at the time her youngest daughter, Emily, was about the same age as Alexis and so was learning the ropes about beach safety and behavior. As my sister sat down, Emily stood impatiently in front of her as she put her daughter's hair up in a hair tie. "Hurry Mom!" Emily fussed, eager to plunge into the cold New Jersey waters on this stiflingly hot day. Finally finished, my sister gave Emily a kiss as she broke free, racing into the water. My sister shouted after her, "Have fun in the water and don't go in too deep!"

We then began to review the events that had happened to our separate worlds since we last saw each other. But it became difficult to have a sustained conversation, as the noise level between my sister and her daughter quickly escalated. Every time my sister noticed that Emily had strayed deeper into the water than she was comfortable, her mother would interrupt our conversation with the phrase, "Just a sec, Steve." And shouting to Emily, "You are in too deep young lady! Come in! You're out too far." The same thing happened when the rip tide pulled Emily closer to the ropes, her mother would yell, "Emily! Get away from the ropes!" And every time Emily did anything her mother disapproved of like throwing sand or shells, her mother would say, "If you don't stop that, young lady, you are going to sit on the beach blanket for five minutes."

This made it impossible to have a conversation, so I decided to watch Alex instead. You know how it is—a father can spend hours watching his five-year-old. She was running and diving in the waves, enjoying herself immensely. Soon she and her cousin Emily were playing together. But after a short while, I began to notice something that struck me.

From time to time, Alex would glance back at the lifeguard stand to make sure she was in the right spot. She also kept an eye on the ropes, making sure she wasn't getting too close. I even saw her intentionally pull

Emily and herself safely away from them. And then, much to my surprise and satisfaction, after a wave crested and broke, I saw Alex look down at her chest to see if she was in too deep. She actually held her hand up to her chest to measure a wave.

Then I noticed that Emily wasn't watching the lifeguard stand, and she wasn't watching the ropes, and she wasn't watching how far from the shore she was. Emily was watching her mom. Every time she thought she might be in too deep or doing something wrong, she would look back at her mom to find out if her behavior was OK. Emily was depending on her mom to determine whether she was in the right spot; Alexis was making that determination herself. Alexis knew what she was doing. And at least for now, on this beautiful, sunny morning, she was keeping herself safe.

Fast forward five years when it was my youngest daughter Maddy's turn to learn the rules of the beach. Just as with Alex, I sat Maddy down to explain the rules including the lifeguard stand, the rope, the waves, and so on. She was eager to get in the water, but I had learned how important this "drill" was in developing a sense of responsibility and letting me relax at the beach.

As I covered the "rules" with Maddy, I felt the stare of my sister, Emily's mom, on the back of my neck. I could sense that she was both curious and perturbed by what she was seeing. After my lecture was over, I freed Maddy to run into the water and turned to my sister. She had a funny, skeptical look on her face.

"What's up?" I asked nicely.

In a frustrated and particularly judgmental tone she proclaimed, "You are such a control freak! Honestly. I don't know how your kids put up with you!"

Introduction

*In the absence of power in a relationship, a person will figure out how
to get it.*

—Anonymous

Which takes more time, managing the activities and behavior of the people who work for you or creating an environment in which they manage
their own behaviors? The answer might surprise you. It also might change
the way you provide direction and coaching to your people. In many
ways and in many circumstances, people managers (and parents) create
dependent behavior in the people they manage without even realizing it.
This causes much unnecessary work and drama, when the alternative is a
pretty simple approach to managing people's performance.

In the current business culture, the most common approach to managing people's performance is something I call "autocratic behaviorism."
This autocratic behavioristic approach to leading and managing people I
define as using positional power or authority to control people's behaviors. Basically, it is practiced by managers as a way of getting people to do
the things they want or need them to do by using the authority inherent
in the manager's organizational position. In other words, by using rank to
get people to perform.

If you think about a time in which you had a difficult relationship
with your manager or supervisor, most likely it was because he or she
tried to control your behavior, most typically with a set of rewards and
punishments.

And the autocratic behavioristic approach worked well in an environment in which managers had the time and authority to make decisions
for their people.

That time has passed.

In the current rapidly paced, just-in-time business world, this approach can often interfere with both productivity and collaboration.

In this world, managers and leaders no longer have the luxury of time, energy, or power to control their people's activities.

Nor do they want to.

This new environment demands that people learn to self-manage and self-motivate. Management's role must change from ensuring people fulfill their duties and achieve their objectives to coaching them to make increasingly smarter and more proficient decisions. This requires a clear shift from trying to control people's behavior to creating an environment in which our people self-manage and self-motivate.

Hands On, Hands Off

People often think of autocratic behaviorism as a micro-managing approach to controlling people's activities. But that is not necessarily the case. This type of controlling management style can be divided into two distinct methods of performance management: hands off and hands on. Both have very different ways of implementing the autocratic-behaviorist approach.

A "hands-on" manager approach is one in which a leader actively engages in controlling behavior from the get-go. This type of management is often described as "micro-managing." It is perceived as controlling because the foundation of this approach is "If you do this, you get that." And "If you don't do this, this is what will happen to you."

When employees perform well, they are rewarded, and when they fail to achieve, they get disciplined. Because this type of manager's behaviors includes enforcing directives, close monitoring, and emphasizing on making sure people "do what they are told," it often frustrates and demotivates good employees.

This demotivating effect is because "micro-managers" tend to focus on factors that are mostly out of their control, like motivation and rewards. (That last statement might startle you, but I will make my case shortly.)

Now the other, and less-effective approach to this autocratic behaviorism is what is sometimes referred to as a "hands-off" management style. A hands-off manager is typically conflict adverse and so avoids engaging with his or her employees until a situation has become too bad to ignore. This type of manager avoids managing until he or she is forced into a situation that is no longer tenable, when a situation can no longer be ignored like an ongoing lack of performance or behavioral issues.

It is unfortunate that many of these managers end up enabling behaviors that if addressed earlier and appropriately would have caused much less disruption and drama.

But when finally forced to deal with a nonperformance issue, these hands-off managers suddenly become very hands on and will use punishment or discipline to "convince" the employee to fall in line. This approach also creates employee resentment and ultimately demotivates the employee to take responsibility and improve performance, at least for the long term.

The autocratic-behaviorist approach for managing performance works well in a hierarchical, highly structured business environment in which roles and responsibilities are static and clearly defined, such as the military, where decision making comes from the top down and obedience is not just expected but mandated.

And until very recently, military and corporate organizational structures mirrored each other. Because the environments were similar, autocratic behaviorism worked well as a management philosophy in both.

Today, however, the role of the corporate manager is rapidly becoming blurred and more difficult to define, much like the structures of today's corporations. The environment and underlying assumptions that once supported the autocratic-behaviorist model have changed. And with a better educated, better informed, and independent millennial work-force, notions of controlling and micro-managing your people are not only outdated, but less and less recognized and rewarded by corporate America. Collaboration, empowerment, and delegation are the true skills of the millennial management.

In the past, management was primarily responsible for making most important and business-critical decisions. But in today's corporations, many of those decisions are made by non-managers out of necessity and the demands of a just-in-time production and performance culture.

Today, the most common management belief in our modern business environment is that decisions are best made by the people closest to the customer. To perform as effectively and efficiently as possible in our hypercompetitive business environment, management needs to shed its command-and-control approach and philosophy, and adopt a much more flexible and cooperative approach to leading others. This belief has impacted management's role.

Add to this the fact that today, most managers are responsible for more people than they would have been in the past. Managers used to be able to count the number of people they were responsible for on one hand. The flatter, leaner, and more responsive corporate model means more individual contributors reporting to fewer managers. This complicates managers' jobs and increased demands on their time and energy.

This changing organizational structure has also impacted a manager's role. Corporate structures are making the transition from stable and predictable top-down hierarchical organizations to flexible and adaptive groups of employees with quickly changing deliverables and priorities, by necessity. With this change, managers are expected to be more flexible as well.

If a manager is going to survive and thrive in this new, complex environment, it will not be by directing his or her people to execute strategies and meet objectives through a control-oriented management approach. In fact, they will be successful only by learning to manage with less and less control.

Shift

As I've said, autocratic behaviorism worked well in an environment in which managers had the time and authority to make decisions for their people. In the current business environment, this approach interferes with success. Managers no longer have the time or power to control employee behavior, nor do they want to. This new environment demands that employees learn to "self-manage."

This shifts management's role from ensuring that people fulfill their duties and meet objectives to helping people take responsibility and make intelligent decisions. This shifts a manager's role from controlling behavior to helping people improve their decision-making processes.

This shift is from autocratic behaviorism to engaged management; from focusing primarily on controlling the behaviors and performance of employees to helping them take responsibility for their own performance and activities. To be successful, managers need to facilitate the process of building confidence in their people's decision-making abilities.

In the autocratic-behaviorist model, managers measure success by the amount of confidence employees have in his or her abilities. An engaged manager measures success by the amount of confidence his or her employees have in their own abilities. In this new environment, a manager's primary responsibility is to help people build confidence in their own expertise and effectiveness.

People who have confidence in their ability to make smart decisions will self-manage. And this in turn becomes self-replicating as people gain more and more confidence because their decisions become better and better. But the challenge in this "facilitative" model is that for people to become confident in their decision making, they must be allowed to make decisions. Management's duty is to help people learn to make smart decisions by creating a safe environment in which people have opportunities to make decisions.

This is not about control. It is about learning. Management's new role is to facilitate the learning process.

So, is the engaged manager a leader or a manager? That depends on where a manager falls in the corporate order. I've worked with very engaged manufacturing line supervisors with great leadership skills, but they are very good people managers. On the other hand, I've worked with extremely disengaged CEOs and other executives who could learn a thing or two about performance management from lower level supervisors and managers. That said, an executive must still focus on performance management, but from a higher, more corporate perspective.

An engaged manager creates and manages the opportunities for employees to learn to become responsible decision makers. The task of building this environment requires a shift in how managers view their job.

A Balance of Profits and Process

The business value most reinforced in American corporate culture is results. While mission, vision, and values all play a role, a publicly traded company will not succeed for long without making money. Management gets rewarded for achieving results and making profits quarter to quarter; that is just how it works.

This emphasis on results has a strong influence on how managers view their job. The dominance of our short-term, results-driven, hyper-capitalistic value system manifests itself in the American "just do it" corporate culture. In this culture, managers see that their primary responsibility is to achieve results. They are measured by things accomplished, objectives met, and deliverables delivered. And this focus is reflected in performance management practices. Management doesn't reward people for day-to-day activities. Management rewards people for meeting objectives, achieving goals, and exceeding expectations.

From this just-do-it culture arises the primary misconception impacting the American management approach: the belief that results can be managed. That setting goals and holding people accountable is managing.

It is not.

The one thing a manager or a person cannot manage is results. Results are either achieved or not achieved; people either meet their objectives and deliverables or they fall short of them. Trying to manage something that has a binary outcome is not possible. No one can manage results. A person can manage only process.

And the mislaid belief that a manager can focus primarily on results and be successful in managing the performance of others is folly. People don't work like that. Managers who struggle with the performance of their people most likely manage by unilaterally setting goals or objectives and holding their people accountable.

This approach has two rather negative longer term effects. First, it can negatively impact a person's motivation. Due to the naturally controlling nature of that approach, it impedes people's ability to think for themselves and self-manage; as in the Alex story, it creates "dependent behavior."

But the largest fault with the autocratic-behavioristic management approach and focus on managing results is that it lets managers off the hook from having to manage performance. Managing people's progress has not traditionally been high on the list of American business values. The overemphasis on achievement allows managers to use results as the measure of how well they are at managing. It becomes self-reinforcing.

This results-focused mentality interferes with a manager's ability to focus on the process of managing.

Let's take sales for instance. As a former sales manager, responsible for the performance of many selling teams, if I just managed my people by whether they made their quota each month, I would be abdicating my responsibility as a manager. And while sales numbers are one indicator of a person's performance in a sales role, there are many other lagging and leading indicators as well. Non-results-centric or metric-based expectations like the number of customer meetings per week a salesperson schedules or the amount of time spent with major influencers, or even the appropriate timeframe for submitting expense reports, all play a part in a salesperson's performance. And as I can tell you from my many years in sales, there are salespeople who make their quota and are still poor performers and others who miss their quotas and are great salespeople. My job is to pay attention to the leading and lagging indicators, not just the numbers.

Another complication of the just-do-it management culture is how managers view performance problems. Managers who define an employee's success by achievement of results will define an employee's failure as falling short of results. Employee performance is rated in terms of achievement, not improvement.

Performance is rated relative to the result, so a manager naturally sees the employee as the source of the performance problem. The employee is perceived as failing, not the management process. The employee, not the manager, has fallen short of the goal.

And when the employee is perceived as the source of the problem, a manager's tendency is to try to "fix" the employee. The default is again to an autocratic-behaviorist approach. Managers who see employees as the problem have no other recourse than to use a control-based approach to try and correct the problem. In the end, employees feel controlled because they are being controlled.

In order to better understand how these approaches differ, and further comprehend the underlying assumptions of each, we will analyze how managers using each approach would attempt to solve a people problem, a problem of nonperformance.

CHAPTER 1

A Performance Problem

Leadership by example is the only kind of real leadership. Everything else is just authority playing itself out.

—Albert Emerson Unaterra

A few years ago, I was asked to take on an employee who was struggling in his role. His name was and is Charles. I did this as a favor to my manager as I had previously salvaged a problematic employee who was now one of the company's top performers. Charles, like the previous employee, was one of the company's poorest performers, and it was my job to turn him around. I knew this was Charles's last chance. If I succeeded in correcting his problems, Charles got to keep his job. If he failed to improve his performance, Charles loses his job.

Prior to meeting with Charles after his lateral move, I reviewed his personnel file to get a handle on the challenges I would face. I wanted to have a game plan for helping him get back on track. I was not encouraged by what I found.

There was a litany of problems recorded by his previous manager. They included:

- He is consistently late for work about 2 days per week.
- He failed to accomplish his objectives in the previous two fiscal years.
- He doesn't return voicemail or e-mail messages for days.
- He constantly bothers other employees when they are busy.
- He shows up late for meetings, even the meetings he calls.
- He invades other people's offices to chat, even when his projects are overdue.
- He refuses to deal with certain employees.

- He has alienated many employees to the point where they no longer deal with him.
- He tends to sabotage his department's efforts by undermining their decisions with other departments.

Where to start, where to start?
I asked myself some questions:

- Is Charles the right person for the job?
- Is he motivated to do the job?
- Why does he seem to create his own problems?
- Does he have an attitude problem?
- Is his personal life interfering with his performance?

When faced with this problem, managers try to figure out whether Charles wants to do the job, and whether he is or isn't motivated to change his behaviors. If Charles isn't motivated, they will then try to "fix" Charles by motivating him. Many managers feel that if a person isn't motivated, there is little that can be done to turn around poor performance. Following this route, managers who fail to motivate Charles will most likely attempt to replace him with someone who is motivated.

The Card Game

This is an exercise I've done with first line supervisors on assembly lines and one-on-one with CEOs in their office suites. I call it the "Card Game" and usually use a set of five cards placed on a table in front of my audience.

The outcome of the Card Game is to get managers to figure out how much control they have over human performance. It is almost always enlightening to every audience.

The best managers are keenly aware of how much control they have over another person's performance. In my experience coaching and working with managers in almost every industry, one key characteristic of all the most successful managers is the ability to focus on the factors they have the most control over; especially when managing and leading people.

And one thing that makes all these managers effective is that they always, always, always focus on the factors they have the most control over; they all manage best within the span of their control.

And the opposite is true as well. Again, in my experience, the managers who are most challenged by people performance issues are those who attempt to control, some might say micro-manage, factors that they have the least control over, regardless of whether theirs is a "hands-on" or "hands-off" approach.

One indicator of whether you as a manager are focusing on the wrong things is the number of performance issues you have in your team. As a manager, you are only as good as your bench strength, and if your bench is causing you problems for more than six months, it might not be the make-up of your team; it might be that you do not understand where your control as a manager starts and where it ends.

So, a good exercise is to apply the factors that you have most control over to apply it to a specific situation, to Charles.

The ability of anyone (in any job) to perform is influenced by five interrelated but independent factors. Managers have more control over some of these factors than others. It is critical to your success as a people manager to understand each of these factors. If you do, then you can begin the work of managing performance without controlling people. As an example, I can salvage Charles's career . . . maybe.

Here are the five factors that impact a person's ability to perform in their role. These are listed in random order, for now.

There is one and only one assumption: that intelligence is a given. Assume, especially in Charles's case, that he is smart enough to perform that task. Charles is a talented guy; he just hasn't been pulling his weight.

So, the question I pose to you is, *Which of these factors do you as a manager have the most control over and which do you have the least control over?*

The answer to that question can determine your success as a people manager.

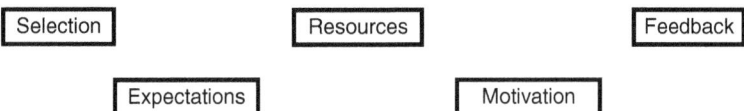

Selection		Resources		Feedback
	Expectations		Motivation	

Before we begin, let me define each one of these factors so you can make a more informed evaluation regarding most control to least control.

Selection: Selection is about hiring and firing; the decision to offer a person a position and the decision to terminate a current employee. So the question is, how much control does a manager have over selection or deselection?

Expectations: Expectations is whether an employee knows what is expected of him or her in the position. These can include many things from job description to professional objectives to code of conduct. Again, how much control does a manager have over an employee's expectations?

Resources: Resources are the tools and support needed to fulfill responsibilities and perform in a role. These can include everything from the needed technology to the proper training. How much control does a manager have over resources?

Motivation: Motivation is the desire to do the job as it is defined. While more qualitative than some of the other factors, it has been proven repeatedly that motivation is key to a person's success in his or her job. So, ask yourself, how much control does a manager have over one of his or her team members' desire to perform?

Feedback: Feedback is the regular coaching and input into performance intended to improve or extend performance. An employee who knows where he or she stands has a better grip on his or her developmental needs and can work on getting better and better. How much control do you as a manager have over feedback?

The next couple of pages may strike you as running counter to many of the leadership/management books you've read or the theories you've heard from business gurus. Keep in mind that my principles come from working with the best leaders, from first-line manufacturing supervisors on Caterpillar assembly lines to executives at United Healthcare, and in almost every other industry.

This comes at you fast, so pay attention.

The six factors that influence performance are listed below in descending order of the amount of control a manager has over them.

Manage Within the Span of Your Control

The factor you as a manager have the most control over is . . .

1. Expectations: *Has the employee been told explicitly what is expected by his or her manager and company?*

You need no one's permission to sit down with your people and have a frank discussion about objectives, deliverables, behavioral guidelines, or anything else that is expected of them. You don't need permission from Human Resources or your manager (although you might want to validate your list of expectations with your direct supervisor) or anyone else.

But then why is it that the most common complaint I encounter from people struggling in their positions is that they do not understand what is expected of them? They almost always complain about unclear, unattainable, or constantly changing priorities. And that contributes to an autocratic behavioristic model of management to "solve" this performance problem.

Why would a manager avoid communicating (engage) and getting buy-in to a set of clearly defined, attainable, flexible, and mutually agreed upon expectations? A couple of reasons.

First, it is the potential for conflict. If the employee fails to buy into any of the proposed objectives or deliverables, a dialogue needs to ensue to work things out. Managers need to be able to communicate, negotiate, and persuade their people into agreeing to expectations up-front.

Second, I would say that many managers have a less-than-complete understanding of the things that are considered expectations. For instance, the following fall under the definition of company expectations: goals and objectives, the company mission, the company vision, the company values, parking policy, compensation policy, behavioral guidelines, work hours, and the list goes on and on.

But there are some key expectations that most employees are interested in having clarified and provide 90 percent of the direction they need. One of the objectives of this book is to clarify them for you and provide tools for reaching a mutually agreed-upon set of expectations that will reduce your people-management challenges and reduce the amount of drama in your team.

But the third and I would say most likely reason managers avoid setting clear expectations is that once a set of mutually agreed-upon expectations are in place, another factor comes into play: accountability. Accountability is the act of applying a consequence; a reward or discipline based on performance. Once an expectation is made clear and agreed upon, if a member of your team falls short of or exceeds, then accountability for his or her performance becomes an inherent part of the expectations. We will address this in much more detail in the following chapters, but keep in mind that without accountability, expectations mean nothing. Once you set a bedtime for your child, you must enforce it. Otherwise that and other rules begin to erode.

Managers who do set expectations often do it in an autocratic way. Expectations can be set as hard-and-fast rules or as guidelines within which people can make their own decisions. Expectations can be set in a way that facilitates the learning process. The way expectations are set can be the starting point for helping people become better decision makers.

My first job is to ensure that Charles is aware of and buys-into the expectations of his job and our company.

The factor that you as a manager have the most control over after expectations are clear is . . .

2. Feedback: *Does the employee know whether he or she is or is not meeting the defined expectations?*

The second most common complaint I hear from individual contributors about their manager is, "I never know where I stand!" And that is also strange because you as a manager need no one's permission to sit down on a regular basis and discuss performance with a person who works for you. You don't have to check with Human Resources or your manager or anyone else for that matter. That is one of the privileges of being a people-manager and one of your responsibilities as a manager and a duty to your people.

Why would a manager avoid providing his or her people with honest and constructive feedback? There are a couple of reasons.

First, many do not know how to have an effective and motivating performance discussion with employees. What comes to mind when you hear these phrases, "First I want to say that you're doing a great job . . ." or "Can I see you in my office for a minute?" or the un-reassuring "First, I'd like for you to tell me how *you* think you are doing." These phrases most likely cause defensive responses from your people or set them up for a demotivating discussion. But it is possible to have an engaged, constructive, and honest discussion if you follow some pretty specific guidelines that we will discuss later.

But the real reason I believe that managers avoid providing honest and constructive feedback to an employee is the challenge of dealing with conflict. Things can get messy if done wrong and too often a dialogue can become an argument, especially when an employee is defensive. For that reason, managers tend to put off performance discussions until they have no choice. And by that time, the only tool they have is to threaten retaliation or discipline, which is a default to autocratic behaviorism, which naturally is seen by an employee as controlling, because it is.

Early intervention, engagement, and follow-through is crucial to avoiding over-controlling and using discipline to correct performance.

Managers owe employees feedback. Without feedback, employees are operating in the dark. And in the absence of regular constructive feedback, employees often create their own. A manager's role is to provide information that allows employees to know how they are doing and whether they are improving.

Charles needs to know where he stands in relation to management's expectations. Without feedback, how can Charles be expected to improve his performance? I quickly discovered that he was clueless when it came to many of them. His previous manager had let him off the hook so often that Charles regarded many of his expectations as suggestions and not actionable offenses.

Most managers who provide feedback do so to control behavior: positive feedback for good behavior and negative feedback for poor behavior. There is an alternative. Feedback can be used as a tool for facilitating a person's learning process instead of to control.

As a manager, once you have fulfilled your responsibilities of reaching agreement on a set of clearly defined expectations and honest, constructive feedback, then the following factors come into play. With that, we can move down the list a bit more quickly.

3. Resources: *Do your people have the tools and resources they need to ensure they can meet expectations?*

Some managers will make the argument that without the proper resources a person cannot be expected to meet expectations. And this is true. But let's come back to the question at hand, which is, how much control do you as a manager have over any of these factors? And while resources are crucial, you have less control over them than expectations and feedback.

All managers have budgets they need to live within and constraints on their spending and capital purchases. This then limits a manager's control over resources. It is the responsibility of managers to fight for and ensure adequate funding and resources for his or her team, but when push comes to shove, budgets get cut all the time. Enough said. With limited resources, a manager must negotiate and defend budget requests as a regular part of his or her job.

And from as far as I could tell, Charles had all the resources he needed to do his job.

Next in line of performance factors that are within a managers' span of control is selection.

4. Selection: *Is the person right for the job?*

Almost immediately I expect, the reader is unhappy with this critical factor occurring this far down the list when it comes to Charles. After all, I had no control over Charles's hiring; he was given to me already an employee. However, selection is about both sides of the coin, both hiring and firing or, more politely, selection and deselection.

And while I had no choice over whether Charles became an employee, I can always get rid of him. That is, if I do it the right way. Managers who have been in the uncomfortable (but not necessarily unpleasant) position of terminating one of their people's employment will tell you, it isn't as simple as just telling a person he or she is done at the end of the day; there is a process that protects all employees from being unfairly terminated while at the same time shielding the company from legal exposure. It's called the Performance Improvement Plan, or PIP. Now, the real purpose of a PIP is to turn around a person's performance in hopes that he or she can continue as a productive member of the team, but too often it becomes a formality of a foregone conclusion that has already been reached.

And the format of PIPs in all corporations is the same, and I've seen them at companies as varied as NIKE, Microsoft, Expedia, Caterpillar, and many others. All PIPs force a manager to document that this person had the opportunity to successfully perform his or her duties by ensuring three things critical to his or her success. Care to take a stab at what those three critical factors might be?

You guessed it. PIPs force a manager to document that the employee was provided with a set of clear *expectations*, regular honest *feedback,* and the *resources* necessary to meeting expectations.

It is a shame that people are provided these more often to help them out the door as opposed to getting them when they first enter the corporate realm.

In today's hectic business environment, many companies take a sink-or-swim view of new employee hiring and development. And of course, this results in some very high performers. But on the other side, I wonder if some of the people who sank could have been good swimmers with better management.

I was not yet to the point of putting Charles on a PIP. While it was an option, for me at least, I had to do right by Charles and make sure he had a shot at keeping his job.

The final performance factor and the one you as a manager have the least control over will surprise and perhaps anger some of you. It is . . .

5. Motivation: *Does this person want to do the job?*

Some of you might strongly disagree with how much control you do or do not have over this factor, but hear me out, please. Motivation is the desire to do a job and is influenced by many work and personal factors.

But as it applies to your control as a manager, you may be able to create an environment in which people motivate themselves, but motivating a person is a tricky and complex skill. Some people quit and leave, while others quit and stay. And for the latter, trying to make them like their job is a thankless and often useless task.

Maslow's Hierarchy of Needs is a nice place to start to understand people's motivation, but it is a poor coaching or performance management tool. People are complex beings with complex needs that vary widely from individual to individual. Managers who ascribe to the "autocratic behaviorist" school of management (even though many don't know that they do) often think that people are mostly driven by a system of rewards and punishments and so default to those to manage and motivate others. This is a very simplistic and insulting approach to managing people.

While Charles does not seem very motivated, I think he needs some time. If I can provide him an environment in which he has clear and attainable goals and regular honest feedback, perhaps his motivation will change for the positive. I don't know, but I should give him a chance.

So, you have a problem with the order I've proposed?

The managers who have the most people problems usually default to the last two of the performance factors listed above as their most trusted and utilized tools for managing the performance of others. When faced with a people issue, I hear these managers tell me, "My job is to find the right people (Selection) and motivate them to do the job (Motivation). And if it turns out that they don't want to do the job, then I'll find someone who does (Selection, or rather deselection)."

The default strategy of relying on factors you have the least control over is a recipe for employee dissatisfaction and people problems. But there are reasons that managers using this strategy to get people to perform find it attractive. First is that it helps them avoid the sometimes difficult work of clarifying expectations, providing ongoing feedback, and ensuring their people have the resources to do their job. In short, it helps them justify their inability or unwillingness to manage.

But the main reason I believe managers default to these two factors is that if you think about it, the manager is never put in the position of being responsible for nonperformance. It's always the employee who is at fault, never the manager. Just listen to the words I most often hear when these managers are asked about their struggling team members, "I don't know. Maybe *they* don't want this job." Or "Maybe *they* were the wrong person to begin with."

It makes it so much easier to hold other people accountable than it is to hold yourself accountable. The hard work of managing is creating an environment in which people self-manage and self-motivate, not one in which people overachieve to get rewarded or live in fear of being disciplined.

The Most Important Performance Factor

So up until this point, I've been fooling you a bit. There is another performance factor I neglected to put on the list. The reason I did this was to make several points that would have seemed less important with this factor in the mix. Another reason is to emphasize how important this factor is to managing performance without controlling people; it is the key to the entire process.

Accountability: *Does this person know what will happen if he or she does or does not perform?*

Lets define terms here before we delve into this factor. First thing to clear up is the definition of the term "accountability." As an action, accountability is the act of applying consequences to performance or nonperformance. For performance that meets or exceeds expectations (there's that word again), employees are rewarded monetarily or by promotion or some other extrinsic reward and recognition. For nonperformance, people are disciplined (think PIP or formal written warnings), denied opportunities for advancement, or ultimately terminated.

I do not use accountability in a theoretical sense, not in this book anyway. Accountability in a performance management sense is the actual act of either warning of or implementing a vehicle for accountability. (Think of the example of threatening a child with a time-out. Until a parent places a child in some time-out space, there is no accountability. Yet.)

But don't confuse accountability with responsibility. Accountability is better thought of as an external consequence, that is, something that is "done to or for a person," while taking responsibility is an internal decision people make; it is something people either accept or reject. You can make a person accountable for some task, deliverable, or role, but it is difficult, if not impossible, to make them feel responsible for any of that. Responsibility is something that is the result of dialogue, discussion, persuasion, and agreement. But ultimately it is a person who takes responsibility freely and not because it is forced on them. Ever tried to hold someone accountable for something they don't think they are responsible for? Now that's a good trick.

The question as to where accountability falls in the order of most-to-least control is almost moot. Because it is such a powerful factor in managing performance, it doesn't matter. What matters is the way in which it helps complete the formula for managing performance without controlling people.

Managers owe employees accountability. This may sound strange, but managers who continually let people off the hook or interfere with the direct consequences of people's actions prevent them from learning. Some managers tend to overuse accountability as a stick to get people to fall in line, while some avoid it at all costs. Both approaches to holding people accountable fall into the autocratic behaviorist model.

If Charles's manager has provided him with a solid basis of clear expectations and frequent feedback, then Charles has chosen to live with the consequences of his actions. Unfortunately, managers who do a poor job of providing clear expectations and feedback often use accountability as a method to control behavior. They substitute accountability for managing.

Accountability can be another tool for people to become better decision makers. It depends on how it is used. For people to become better decision makers, they must have the opportunity to make decisions and experience the direct consequences of those decisions. Facilitating the learning process means providing a safe environment for people to make decisions and experience consequences. It means helping people to hold themselves accountable.

At this point the reader might be hesitant to accept the order of these factors. That is natural. This resistance comes from the tendency in this country to focus on outcome and not process, our "just do it" culture. The outcome I want from the Charles management challenge is an employee who is right for the job and motivated. How I get Charles to successfully perform his job responsibilities is the process.

Because of the focus on outcomes rather than process, managers address problems after they have occurred, not before. This focus influences how managers see and deal with performance problems. They most often see the employee and not themselves as the problem. Upon seeing the person as the problem, managers try to correct it by attempting to motivate.

This strategy of trying to motivate employees, and if unsuccessful hiring someone else, is another attempt to manage results, not process. All managers want employees who are right for the job and motivated. Managers believe they have the most control over these two factors: selection and motivation. They attempt to manage performance problems by trying to motivate employees and, failing that, look for someone who can and will do the job. Managers think they can avoid the responsibility of managing if they hire qualified, motivated people.

Managers who attempt to control behavior will place their emphasis on accountability to get people to do what they want. These managers see their role in providing clear expectations and frequent feedback as less important than accountability.

The facilitative leader sees that his or her primary responsibility is to provide expectations and feedback. Doing a good job of clarifying expectations and giving feedback reduces the need to hold people accountable.

In general, managers in this country emphasize accountability over expectations and feedback. Recently a trend has developed for managers to engineer more accountability into the workplace. There are three reasons for this increasing emphasis on accountability.

The primary reason is the "just do it" management approach. This puts primary emphasis on results, not process. Managers are good at identifying goals and objectives but not very good at clarifying expectations and providing feedback. Unfortunately, this ability interferes with managing the progress toward achieving those goals. Management-by-objectives is not managing; it is goal setting and yet another attempt to manage results.

Second, most managers are unclear on their roles and responsibilities. Corporations send their managers to leadership seminars before they have the skills to do an effective job of managing. It is very difficult to become a good leader without management skills. With the increase in authority that people get when promoted into management goes an increase in responsibility to the people they manage. When managers only see the increase in authority without feeling the increased responsibility, they will use accountability to exercise that authority.

The third reason managers focus on accountability to manage is the fast-paced, results-focused environment they work in. This environment encourages management by exception. The squeaky wheel gets the oil. Managing by exception focuses on solving problems after they have occurred. Managers naturally see the employee as the cause of the problem.

A person who is interested in facilitating the learning process builds the groundwork for people to make decisions. He or she first realizes the increased responsibility, then the increased authority.

The first and most important step for facilitating the learning process is to provide clear expectations. Expectations create the base camp from which people can push themselves to greater heights. Expectations provide the net that makes it safe to take risks. Facilitative leaders accept the responsibility of ensuring that people have a good foundation for achievement.

The second most important step of facilitating the learning process is to frequently provide feedback. Feedback helps people manage their own progress. Facilitative leaders spend time giving feedback about how a person is improving or slipping in their progress. This feedback is process based more than results based. Results-based feedback identifies whether an employee has or hasn't achieved an objective. Process-based feedback reinforces specific behaviors that are or are not working. Using the base camp analogy, reaching the summit is a good goal, but most people appreciate help determining the best equipment and route to get to the top.

When a solid base of expectations exists and people know how they are doing in relation to those expectations, then accountability becomes a natural part of the process. As people become more confident in their decision-making abilities, they are more likely to hold themselves accountable. Facilitative leadership doesn't mean holding people accountable. It means helping people hold themselves accountable. A leader doesn't try to make people responsible; he or she helps people take responsibility.

Shifting away from an autocratic behaviorist approach is not accomplished by doing different things. It is achieved by shifting the primary emphasis away from the employee's actions to the manager's responsibilities in helping or hindering a person's success. Facilitating learning means focusing on the parts of the process that managers have control over and are responsible for providing to their employees. The manager looks first in the mirror for the source of the problem.

The difference between an autocratic behaviorist approach and that of the facilitative leader can be illustrated in the models below. A manager who attempts to control behavior uses accountability as his or her primary tool. Feedback is usually in the form of a performance appraisal or infrequent "constructive" criticism. Expectations are assumed.

Facilitating learning requires a different emphasis than a control-based approach. The facilitative leader sees his or her primary role as communicating, clarifying, and coming to agreement on the boundaries within which all employees are expected to work. Feedback is process and results based. When clear, agreed-upon expectations exist and prompt, frequent feedback has been given, employees hold themselves accountable. Facilitative leaders get themselves out of the way.

This shift in emphasis also requires a different way of providing expectations, feedback, and accountability. Managers can provide these three factors to their people in a way that doesn't attempt to control them. Before we move on to this topic, it is important to clarify how much control

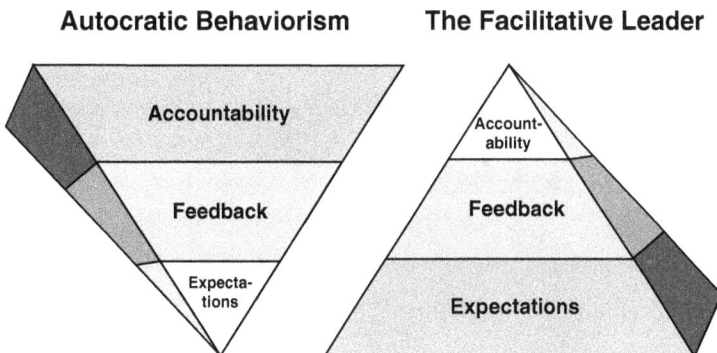

Autocratic Behaviorism

Accountability

Feedback

Expecta-tions

The Facilitative Leader

Account-ability

Feedback

Expectations

managers have over the three remaining performance factors: resources, selection, and motivation. In the remaining chapters, we will use Charles to contrast a management approach that emphasizes control to one that facilitates learning. Chapter 2 will examine expectations and how managers can create either an environment in which people self-manage or one that reinforces management-dependent behavior. Chapter 3 identifies the different effects of results-based and process-based feedback. In the fourth chapter, two different methods for helping people hold themselves accountable are presented.

The final chapter deals with the problem of empowerment. It illustrates how today's corporate environment works against empowerment and provides a game plan for moving to an empowered workplace. The objective of the rest of this book is to help managers shift from trying to control behavior to helping people improve their decision-making skills.

To make this shift, managers will need to focus on the three critical performance factors: expectations, feedback, and accountability.

A famous conductor once said, "When I have a problem with the orchestra, I come down off my podium, walk into my dressing room and look in the mirror. I usually find the source of the problem staring back at me."

This statement embodies the mindset of the *facilitative leader*.

The Facilitative Leader

A

I know what will happen if I perform or do not perform

F

I know where I stand

I know what is expected

E

CHAPTER 2

Expectations

High achievement always takes place in the framework of high expectation.

—Charles Kettering

Hey Steve. I wanted to take the time to welcome you to the company and tell you how excited we are to have you onboard.

Thanks. I'm really happy to be part of the team.

Well, you've made a great decision to join us and I wanted to take some time up front to clarify a couple of things. That okay with you?

Of course. Being on the same page I think is the best way to start my career here.

Couldn't have said it better myself. So, let me tell you a bit about my management style. Still good?

Absolutely!

Well, the first thing I want to share with you, and in fact I think you will be happy with, is that I am a hands-off manager.

Okay. What does that mean?

It means that we hired you because you are a smart guy and a go-getter.

Yes, I've always been proud of my past accomplishments.

And we are paying you really great money and giving you really great benefits.

And I appreciate that.

So my approach is to support your efforts, whatever they may be.

Can you be a bit clearer, please?

So let me cut through the BS and just tell you what I want from you, okay?

I'm all ears.

I expect you to go out and figure out what needs to be done as quickly as you can. Then I want you to work hard and get as much done as you can. I support your efforts unequivocally and am excited to see what you come up with.

Okay.

So get out there and create your future. I am excited about your future with our company.

Is there anything else?

Good question. Yes, one more thing. I am known around here as a motivator and I am proud of that label. I expect you to have a good attitude and a can-do approach.

Okay.

And because I don't want you to feel as though I'm leaving you out there totally on your own, we'll meet from time-to-time to course-correct. Got it. . . . Great!

I'm not sure I fully understand . . .

I assure you that you will. OJT takes time, get it?

Well, can we talk about specifics?

Hey Steve. Don't crash my high so soon. You're not becoming 'high maintenance' already, are you?

Well, I . . .

Cool. Hey, gotta run to another meeting. I'm already twenty minutes late. Like I said, unconditional support. Later Gator.

All too often, a dialogue like this is the standard operating procedure to welcome new employees. And it immediately creates problems, some of which are unforeseen and unanticipated.

For one, the responsibility for understanding and accomplishing the things that are expected rests solely on the new employee. If something goes wrong, then it gets blamed on the new employee, not the manager/leader. After all, this person's manager provided direction, right? Just figure out what needs to be done.

But if the new person makes a mistake or confuses priorities, it never becomes the lack of clarity of expectations. So, it is never the manager who is at fault; it is always the employee.

And on another note, sometimes, despite unclear expectations, an employee may be a "quick study" and get most things right. And that's great, except for the fact that most of the time he or she had to figure things out on a trial-and-error basis, which is less effective and less efficient than if he or she had clearer direction.

And the fact that this laissez-faire approach works sometimes feeds the belief that a "hands-off" management approach is effective. But this conclusion fails to consider how many people just "didn't get it" who could have "gotten it" with a bit more clarification from his or her manager. Or even how much time and effort a new hire had to expend that could have been saved by a bit more coaching.

But the ends justify the means, right?

So, this makes the first and most important question regarding the management dilemma and Charles, which is: "Does Charles know explicitly what is expected of him by his manager and company? Is he or was he clear on what was and is expected of him?"

So there I was, one hour before my first meeting with Charles. This would be my first opportunity to begin the process of attempting to turn around his performance. His previous manager had a confidential file where he kept notes on Charles's issues and challenges. It wasn't a personnel file per se, but more of an informal collection of notes, none of which had been documented in an HR written warning or anything like that. Which meant that despite these cryptic notes, there was no paper trail of incriminating evidence I could use in case things with Charles didn't go as I was hoping they would. So, I was basically starting from scratch, which in a way was the best for both Charles and me, no assumptions from me and a clean slate for him.

I wanted to make sure to address the issues that will impact Charles and his contribution to the department the most. In his file, I identified three complaints that seemed simple enough to remedy and a good initial indicator of how difficult this project would become. First, Charles is consistently late for work an average of two days out of each month. Coworkers complain that this behavior interferes with their ability to hold early meetings. Also, those who depend on Charles's work are upset that they can't reach him at critical times. Second, Charles doesn't return voicemail messages for days. When he does finally answer them, he often leaves incomplete or abrupt answers. Third, Charles only partially met his objective last year of introducing two new products to the market. He did introduce one new product, but it didn't meet customer requirements. He never got around to introducing the second product.

Charles's previous manager left some notes in Charles's file concerning his responses to these problems. Regarding his chronic lateness, Charles is a single parent and has a problem with his daycare. The daycare sometimes falls through and he must make last-minute arrangements.

About the voicemail issue, Charles feels overworked. When his manager tried to hold him accountable, Charles pointed out that it sometimes took his manager a long time to answer voicemail messages. Charles also indicated that he likes to wait until he has all the information necessary before returning messages.

When asked why he introduced only one product to the market during the previous year, Charles said that the marketing department didn't get the research data to him in time to introduce more than one product. Additionally, he stated that the product that was introduced met all the internal specifications before release. He felt that it wasn't his fault if the market research was wrong.

As Charles's manager, where do I start? How do I define and clarify expectations for Charles without controlling him? How do I use expectations to facilitate the learning process while meeting my own objectives?

To answer these questions, we must look at the underlying assumptions managers have about expectations.

Understanding Expectations

Most managers do a poor job of communicating expectations. They often assume that people should know the proper rules of conduct and the usual lines of communication. In addition, many "hands-off" managers believe that everyone has or should have the same value system as they or their company. Another contributing factor may be that managers find it easier to manage by exception to avoid potential conflicts that might arise from defining expectations. The last reason managers do a poor job of setting expectations is that they often don't know what they need to communicate.

In addressing the first reason, it is important to realize that assumptions can quickly become problematic. As anyone who has had to defend the firing of an employee knows, the first and most important question asked by legal counsel is "Did you explicitly tell your employee that this was part of his or her job?" The manager should answer that question with a simple "yes" or "no." Assumptions won't work. So, poor management approaches can increase a company's legal exposure and complicate hiring and terminating practices.

Managers who avoid setting expectations due to fear of potential conflict may do so because of their own underlying belief system. If managers perceive expectations as rules and regulations established by management and imposed upon employees, then it is understandable that they avoid them. If, however, managers perceive and set expectations as guidelines that are mutually agreed upon from the start, and implemented to facilitate efficient work processes, then there is less of a reason to fear conflict. Rules and regulations are meant to control; guidelines are intended to provide just enough direction to help people make decisions.

Lastly, if managers avoid communicating expectations because they don't know what to communicate, then the rest of this chapter should help.

But before we move on, one question needs to be answered: When managers avoid setting expectations, where and from whom do employees get them? They get them from many different sources.

The most influential source of employee expectations is the behavior of other employees, including managers. From observing behaviors people assume that if it is permissible for one person then it must be permissible for everyone. Recent business scandals in the United States point to a breakdown in a company culture that is communicated more by management behavior and reward systems than by the mission and vision statements "on the wall."

Even though a company may have the best set of corporate values and vision set out in the company handbook or posters in the hallways, it is the inappropriate and even illegal behavior employees see every day that sabotage those same corporation's values and vision. "Do as I say, not as I do" is no excuse and is not legally defensible, as we have seen in some of the recent corporate meltdowns.

When people develop their own set of expectations based on observation, they often reinforce the behaviors that most satisfy their needs and not necessarily those in the best interest of the organization. That is human nature.

Employees develop their expectations from previous managers as well. This can be good or bad, depending on the previous manager's ability to set expectations that meet organizational needs. And especially today with the multicultural and global business environment, people bring into the workplace their cultural background, work history, and personal beliefs. These factors also influence expectations. If managers do not set clear expectations, people will develop their own set of assumptions.

In Charles's example, he may believe he did everything in his power to meet expectations that he assumed were correct. If his manager did not clarify and obtain agreement to the expectations beforehand, Charles won't feel responsible. And as anyone would, if he does not feel responsible, there is no way he will hold himself accountable.

Standards or Goals?

In the corporate world, expectations can be broadly characterized as falling into two categories: standards and goals. Standards are general expectations of conduct that help businesses function in an efficient manner. A set of mutually agreed-upon standards help companies provide direction for day-to-day behavior and conduct.

Standards cover everything from things as basic as work hours, drug, and alcohol policy and vacation policy to the complexities of the company vision and mission. I am often asked the difference between leadership and management. And I point out that from a manager's perspective, the more basic standards like code of conduct and work hours are more likely to be the domain of first-line supervisors and middle management. But mission, vision, and values are also expectations, and while not always considered "management" in the true sense, they do create an environment specific to a particular company and organization.

The purpose of goals or objectives (I use the words interchangeably at least in this book) is intended to stretch individuals, departments, and corporations into the future. Goals make groups and individuals push themselves to rise higher, to become and attain more than they can in their day-to-day activities. In short, standards are process-focused, while goals are future-focused.

One problem I often run into is the overemphasis on goals and objectives. In a results-driven culture, goals take precedence over standards almost all the time. But when you think about it, the most common reason employees are terminated, especially at the first-line to middle management level, is standards being violated, and not falling short of goals or objectives. But goals without standards become demotivating. When managers neglect the process of identifying and coming to agreement on standards, they overlook the first step in facilitating the learning process.

As previously stated, standards can be perceived as rules and regulations or guidelines. The more a manager sees his or her job as controlling behavior, the more likely he or she is to dictate or avoid setting standards. Often this type of manager will try to extrinsically motivate people to change unproductive behavior through goal setting.

Bryce and Genie Industries

You may not have ever heard of Genie Industries, but most of you know their products. On any given day, on any given construction site, there are multiple what are called "aerial work platforms" or as sometimes referred to as "cherry pickers." One of the best-selling and most reliable is made by Genie Industries. They refer to it as a Genie Lift. These cherry pickers can reach as high as 180 feet in the air.

Genie was founded by a couple of University of Washington graduates in the 1970s, and its growth has been phenomenal mostly due to their incredible quality and excellent leadership. Several years ago, I was brought in to establish an "engaged" management culture throughout the entire company. Despite a fairly enlightened and respected leadership team, employee turnover and other personnel issues were increasingly causing middle management problems.

After taking the executive team through the "Card Game," they concluded that lack of clear expectations and regular feedback might be the core issues. The company decided they liked my approach so well (expectations/feedback/accountability) that anyone who manages people should go through a short one-day workshop. So for more than a year, I lead everyone from the CEO to first-line supervisors through the program.

After the initial training launch, I continued to consult with individual managers struggling with day-to-day management of their team. At one point, a first-line production supervisor named Bryce contacted me for some advice. He said that having attended the workshop, he was inspired to embrace the principles and wanted to show me a "tool" he created to help manage his team. Now keep in mind that Bryce had never had any previous management/leadership training and had a 12-year history at Genie. I was flattered that someone so experienced would find a new way to use my ideas.

Here is what Bryce came up with and began using with his team. He called it his "Expectation Letter" and related that it was very much helping to straighten out his team's performance issues.

Expectations Letters

Author: First Shift Manufacturing Line Supervisor

First Shift Services Team Member

What you can expect from me:

- *I will give you 100 % in heart and effort*
- *Clear expectations, timely feedback and fair accountability*
- *To listen and help resolve problems and issues*
- *Provide the necessary resources to accomplish our goals safely and on time*
- *Provide an environment where your ideas and concerns can be heard and discussed with team members and myself*
- *That I will ask you why until we find the root of the problem then set out to correct it*
- *Provide and environment which encourages education and learning*
- *To relentlessly pursue "Continuous Improvement" throughout our work area*
- *I will follow company policy and in doing so help to create an environment based on true teamwork*

What I expect from you:

- *To make safety your highest priority*
- *That you treat all other team members with the same respect and trust that you would want*
- *To meet production goals while upholding quality standards*
- *To support team decisions; it is your right to disagree but support all decisions based on the good of our team*
- *To cross train in all areas*
- *To pursue your career goals with focus*
- *Do what you say you will do*
- *To leave a clean work area with all tools stored in their place for the next shift*
- *To provide adequate notice when you will be absent or late*
- *To find you in your work area on time and ready to get the job done*
- *To fill in for absent team members when required to do so*
- *To let me know early if you do not have the material or will not meet production in the time allowed*
- *To aggressively attack all forms of waste*
- *To be an effective problem solver; present solutions not just problems*
- *Embrace the principles of "Lean Manufacturing" and actively use and promote its processes*
- *To know your customer needs and meet them*
- *To understand and follow all company policies as laid out in the Team Members Handbook*

Date: _____

Team Member Name: _____

Team Member Signature: _____

Supervisor Signature: _____

Bryce's Expectation Letter format was a stroke of genius. The idea of starting with the things his team could expect from him set a great tone and communicated his belief that both managers and individual team members are accountable. I next noted that the list of expectations was longer for team members than for Bryce. Not a big problem, but you can see how that might be perceived as authoritarian.

As of that day, all managers at all levels at Genie Industries have an agreement with their teams in the form of an Expectation Letter. And since the company is in the construction industry, it is expected that team members sign-on as a commitment or contract with their managers and company.

Another thought I had upon reading this was that Bryce's Expectation Letter contained only standards, no objectives.

I asked him how he used this in his day-to-day management activities, and he told me that he uses it most often for new hires. With his current team, he sat down with each individually and reviewed it. Of course, signing it was a bit of negotiation with some, but he positioned it not so much as an accountability tool as much as a communication document.

He also shared with me an unexpected, but, I think, positive result. Now whenever Bryce has a performance discussion with one of his people, they give him feedback on his performance as well. His team members often bring their copy of the Expectation Letter to performance reviews and discussion.

Bryce says that this has made him a better manager and eliminated a number of less-than-desirable behaviors and ultimately improved morale.

So, after this experience, I began to show Bryce's Expectation Letter to my clients in other industries at differing levels of management. Many CEOs admired Bryce's work and developed their own set of "expectations" for their team. IT leaders, construction supervisors, sales managers, and executives, using Bryce's as a template, developed their own Expectation Letters for their teams.

This example was developed by a sales manager of a large software company in the Seattle area.

Sales Representative Expectations

What I expect from you:

- Deliver results by meeting quarterly financial goals
- Take initiative and ownership in regards to your job responsibilities

- Understand and use the five-step sales process as laid out by Steve for each client including blue printing, cold calling, presentations, customer management review and Opportunity Map
- Accurately update all Sales information for your clients by end of business Friday including notes about activity in each account you contacted that week. All info in Salesforce.com must be current
- Demonstrate a strong ability to understand and articulate the business needs of your prospects, existing clients and industry within your territory
- Provide me prompt communication ear-to-ear about issues and problems before they escalate into unmanageable situations; no surprises
- Can present, articulate and demonstrate all features, value and benefits of our products and services
- Focus on selling the Consulting end of the business
- Commit to your continuing education by attending training and internalizing and applying all skills
- You are expected to win when engaged and be prepared to explain your losses and a game plan for preventing them in the future
- Present issues and problems outlining circumstances, recommendations and potential solutions
- Provide leadership and example to your fellow employees through your work ethic, attitude and fiscal responsibilities by adhering to our Corporate and Sales policies

What you can expect from me:

- Frequent communication of our mission, values and corporate direction
- Assistance and guidance in achieving your goals and meeting expectations
- The opportunity to discuss and clarify my expectations of you
- Weekly feedback on your performance relative to my expectations
- Timely attention to your issues and challenges to help you successfully fulfill your responsibilities
- To go to bat for you when we mutually agree upon a plan of action

- Push ownership, responsibility and credit to you
- Establish support training and educational opportunities for your career development
- Provide value by assisting you in developing your account strategies and tactics as we review your funnel activity
- To travel to targeted or problem accounts when given sufficient notice

As you can see, this example has much more detail than Bryce's letter and clearly oriented toward a sales environment. And in this industry, there isn't a need for a signature if the salespeople agree to commit to these expectations.

This next one comes from an executive in a computer networking company in the San Francisco Bay area.

Author: Executive Vice-President of Global Customer Support for Optical Networking Company

Customer Service and Support Clarification Memo
What you can expect from me:

- All that I expect of you
- To communicate management decisions on a timely basis
- Provide clear expectations and an opportunity to discuss
- To hold you and your team accountable to all deliverables, milestones and behavior
- Guide you to help solve you and your team's problems/issues
- Push ownership, accountability and credit to you
- To create an environment where constructive disagreement, questions and teamwork are encouraged
- Provide you with my rationale for decisions that do or do not support/fund your requests or proposals
- Timely attention to your issues and challenges
- To provide leadership and examples to the rest of the Customer Support organization through my work ethic, attitude, commitment, honesty and teamwork
- Paging—Response within 15 minutes for critical issues

- Voice mail—same business day
- Email—within 24 hours if not traveling

What I expect of you:

- To weigh quality and customer satisfaction more heavily than cycle time and CS revenue
- To use personal initiative to continue to add to your technical and product expertise
- When in doubt to error on the side of the customer—both internal and external. Look at all issues from their perspective
- To take personal ownership and initiative if you see a problem— regardless of functional area or organization. Solve it if you can, escalate it to the proper level if you can't and follow up to ensure resolution and closure
- To internalize and evangelize that one of Customer Supports' role is to help sell more product
- To motivate your team to become champions of product quality
- Present issues and problems outlining circumstances, recommendations and several potential solutions
- Continuously strive to broaden you and your teams' perspective to include areas outside of your functional area
- To establish meaningful and realistic personal goals and objectives and review them on a quarterly basis
- To set reasonable but aggressive business goals
- Communicate to me in person if you will miss a deadline as soon as it is clear you will miss it
- To continuously strive for performance improvement and delivery innovation—establish a new paradigm. Make us "legendary"
- To provide leadership and examples to the rest of the Customer Support organization through your work ethic, attitude, commitment, honesty and teamwork
- To solicit feedback regularly
- Paging—Response within 15 minutes for critical issues
- Voice mail—same business day
- Email—within 24 hours if not traveling

Areas evaluated at Yearly Review

- Technical Skills
- Teamwork
- Interpersonal Skills
- Planning and Organizing
- Professionalism
- Decision Making Skills
- Leadership
- Adapting Skills
- Business Knowledge

This manager even went to the level of detail on response time, which as you can imagine in a customer service role is critical. The addition of the key review areas that tie the document to the yearly performance appraisal process is a nice touch.

How to Effectively Use an Expectation Letter

First, in most companies unilaterally developing a set of expectations and e-mailing them to your team is *not* recommended. A manager should give careful consideration not just to the list of expectations but how best to communicate them in a collaborative and respectful manner. If you have an experienced team with few issues, a more collaborative approach works best. A tenured employee might get the idea that he or she isn't currently meeting expectations without some explanation.

One of the best demonstrations of leadership I experienced was with a VP of sales for Bay Networks (a networking hardware manufacturer) when I attended a meeting with him in France. I had recently shown him the Card Game, and he got the idea of expectations/feedback/account-ability and bought completely into the idea of clear expectations as a tool for creating self-managing employees.

In a conference room with his 12 direct reports, he asked them a simple question, "What is it that you think I expect of you?"

To which they all replied, "To hit our numbers!" To which he asked again, "No, really. What do you think I expect from you?"

The sales executives all stared at him in a confused way. And their boss said, "Well, that's a good place to start."

And he spent the next two hours discussing and agreeing on a set of mutually agreed-upon, realistic, and clear expectations they could all live with and become accountable to. Impressive.

Which looked like this:

Author: Vice-President of Sales for Technology Company

Regional Manager Performance Expectations

A) Business Volumes (Weight 50 percent)
- Quota—achieve 100 percent of your annual assigned revenue goals. Effectively utilize all company resources including SE's, AE's, OS, Corporate HQ, Regional Support Team and any other resources required to accomplish your goals
- Forecast—provide a monthly summary of anticipated sales over the next 90 days using 3 Month Revenue Forecast and the Top 20 format. Accuracy should be within a range of −10 to +25 percent on a quarterly basis
- Pricing—review account activity to ensure that the proper discount category has been used, and if necessary manage the account towards the proper pricing level

B) Territory Management (Weight 20 percent)
- Geographic Management—Actively develop the potential in each territory within your region for all products and services. Utilize the proper mix of company and third party resources to insure territory coverage, account penetration, relationship management and customer satisfaction
- Document, distribute and ensure follow up on all leads generated by Marketing. Monitor customer satisfaction numbers generated by technical support
- Account Targeting—within each territory identify Target Account opportunities and develop a plan to establish an account relationship. Actively utilize the Advanced Sales Process as designed by Steve and Performance Focus. Provide specific management focus on competitive accounts

C) Personnel Management (Weight 15 percent)

- Performance Plans—develop a Performance Appraisal Plan for each employee and review the plans at the beginning of each year. These plans must be specific, realistic and measurable. Conduct quarterly and annual reviews on a timely basis
- Employee Management—actively work with non-performing employees to ensure they are receiving maximum assistance in improving their performance. However, where improvement is not occurring take decisive and documented steps with the assistance and guidance of Human Resources to manage the employee out of the business

D) Expense Management (Weight 5 percent)

- Territory Travel, Entertainment and other Business Expenses—conduct your business in a prudent manner and manage your Regional Expense Budget to minimize Sales Expenses without sacrificing business volume. Ensure expense reports are submitted on a weekly basis

E) Personal (Weight 5 percent)

- Development—establish a set of personal goals to improve your professional and technical skills. Prepare plan with specific objectives and recommendations by June 30 and review with your manager

F) Other (Weight 5 percent)

- Company Knowledge—be the company corporate spokesperson for your region and can present the Corporate Strategy/Vision and relating key advantages and benefits of our products and company in terms that a customer executive can understand
- Communications—use voice mail, email, and other established communication systems to make sure you and your staff are aware of product developments, announcements and requests for information. Use the monthly Operations Report to effectively communicate with other managers
- Confidentiality—recognize that much information (i.e. customer names and contacts, order rates and discounts, product development and release schedules, new products, etc.) provided to you to accomplish your job is considered confidential. Use this

information carefully for Regional and account planning purposes. Do not disclose confidential information to anyone outside the company without specific approval of your direct Vice-President

- Company Assets—recognize that you manage and have access to significant company physical and information assets. Use these assets to improve your productivity and professional presentation of our company and our products. Manage the information assets carefully by providing security and establishing backup procedures as required.

Whether you decide to develop your set of expectations as a team or on your own, it is important that you go through the exercise. Having them clear in your own mind allows you to remind and reinforce them in your daily management activities.

More about Standards

The first responsibility a manager has to his or her people is to communicate and agree upon clear standards. Standards are general expectations of conduct that help to facilitate business processes and decisions. Standards establish guidelines within which employees can make decisions. Standards address day-to-day activities and how people conduct themselves.

Unlike goals, employees are not rewarded for meeting standards. If the standards are agreed upon, realistic, and measurable, then people are held accountable to them. Without clear standards, it is impossible and unfair to hold people accountable.

A manager helps create an environment for learning by coming to agreement on a code of conduct with his or her employees. Managers will have the most success holding people accountable to standards that are realistic, measurable, and agreed upon.

Accountability . . . again!

Expectations need to be realistic if people are going to buy into them. People will not hold themselves accountable or feel responsible for unrealistic expectations. If management defines expectations that are unrealistic, management will be responsible for holding people accountable. If employees do not buy into expectations, management will be forced to use an autocratic-behaviorist approach to keep employees "in line."

Effective expectations are better when they are behavioral, but they don't necessarily need to be. For instance, a company's set of values are typically not behavioral. Values like respect, cooperation, and continuous improvement don't tell employees how to behave. They do, however, provide guidelines for conduct, decision making, and other behaviors.

Behavior expectations like a code of conduct can be observed and measured. Telling an employee to be a better "team player" sends the wrong message even if the manager's intentions are noble. Usually, terms like this can be broken down into behaviors if you simply give it enough thought.

One manager made this exact complaint about one of his people to me so I helped him clarify it in the behavior of this person. "What is it that he does that makes you think he is not a team player?" I asked. "He just doesn't support the team in a way that makes us look like we are on the same page."

"You said, 'in a way.' Can you give me an example of this?" He thought for a while before finally realizing. "So here is what he does. We have these team meetings to discuss progress on our deliverables and goals for each month. And he never says anything, but when we think we have all agreed I find out later that he told another person outside of our group that he thinks we have made a mistake."

"Got it. Here is the behavioral expectation that should fix that: In our team meetings, we all respect the right to disagree. But once we reach agreement we present all decisions as team decisions. And if anyone disagrees it is his or her responsibility to hash it out either in a group or one-on-one. We are a united front."

Clear standards that make sense to employees help build a foundation for learning. An ambiguous standard can demotivate employees, especially if the manager is responsible for defining what behavior falls within the standard.

For example, let's say a standard exists for all employees to have a good attitude. If the manager is the judge of what is or isn't considered a good attitude, then employees will feel that they have little control over what behaviors fall within the desired standard. This can demotivate. A better standard might be for people to leave their personal problems out of business discussions.

Agreement on standards is the key difference between autocratic behaviorism and facilitative leadership. Managers who believe they are "in charge" will most often define and communicate standards unilaterally to their people. Excluding people from control over rules they are expected to live by will affect the amount of responsibility they take for them. By forcing standards on people, managers may get compliance but rarely commitment.

Standards can be broken down into formal and informal. Formal standards are rules to ensure a safe, effective company environment, while informal standards are the tools managers can use to facilitate the learning process.

Formal Standards

Formal standards are defined either by the company or by government regulations and apply to the entire organization. An example of a formal company standard may be standardized work hours. A formal government standard is the OSHA requirement to wear hard hats in construction sites. Formal standards establish a safe and effective corporate environment within which all employees must operate.

Formal standards are usually codified and printed in a company handbook. It is the company's and the individual manager's responsibility to ensure that all employees are aware of these standards.

Managers can communicate formal standards as rules and regulations or as guidelines identified by the company and government to facilitate processes and protect people. While managers have little direct control over formal standards, they can control how they are communicated.

Informal Standards

Informal standards are the guidelines an individual manager and his or her employees have identified as necessary to accomplish day-to-day tasks. They are within the manager's span of control. Informal standards are best defined and agreed to collaboratively by the people who are expected to live by them. Informal standards help build an environment that reflects the department's business and personal values. Examples include guidelines for holding meetings, how conflicts are resolved, and general communication ground rules.

While job descriptions are individual standards and define what is expected of employees, informal standards define how employees are expected to fulfill their responsibilities in the context of working with others.

It is a manager's responsibility to ensure that all his or her employees understand and agree to these standards. Managers ultimately have the authority to define and implement standards, but to encourage people to make their own decisions, it is critical that managers get their people to help define and agree to standards.

An autocratic-behaviorist manager will dictate standards he or she feels are important without getting input from the people who are expected to live by them. A facilitative leader lets his or her group define the most important areas in which standards facilitate work processes. Then he or she allows the people affected by the standard work out the guidelines to improve these processes.

To collaboratively define standards, it is critical to know the difference between rules and guidelines.

Rules vs. Guidelines

Many managers see standards as hard-and-fast rules that they are supposed to enforce. Facilitative leaders see them as guidelines for decision making. The purpose of rules is to control. The purpose of guidelines is to guide.

Rules are normally set in the context of what isn't allowed without any indication of what is allowed. They tend to limit the amount of judgment a person has to use to evaluate compliance to the rule. Rules limit the choice to either compliance or noncompliance.

Guidelines allow judgment and choice by the person expected to live within them. Broad guidelines give people a wider range of choices, and therefore, people will need to exercise more judgment. Narrow guidelines provide less choice and judgment.

Formal standards are more likely to be set as hard-and-fast rules because the consequences of violating them can have a severe impact on others. A strict Drug and Alcohol policy is an example of a formal standard in the form of a rule. The consequences of an employee showing up to work under the influence of drugs or alcohol and then operating heavy machinery can be severe. Some rules are necessary to ensure that a business functions properly.

But too many unnecessary rules can interfere with a manager's ability to be effective. Using effective guidelines instead of rules in certain situations may save a manager time and help employees learn. Informal standards are the best tools managers have to help people become better at making decisions.

We can use a parenting analogy to illustrate how a standard can be used in a way to help people learn. Parents who see their primary responsibility as ensuring that their children obey may define a rule like, "No bike riding in the street." This only tells the child what he or she cannot do. Using this rule when the child rides into the street, the parent will hold the child accountable by taking away his or her bike-riding privileges. This is seen by the child as punishment, which it of course is.

Parents who see their primary responsibility as helping children learn will define guidelines like "You may ride your bike in the driveway until you can ride without falling down. Then you can ride in the street." The child will then practice learning how to ride before approaching the parent to ride in the street. Which approach will the child be more motivated to follow?

In the first example, the parent will spend time monitoring whether the child is in the street. In the second, the parent will spend time tracking the child's learning process.

A comparison can be drawn between the parent and the manager. Telling employees what they can and cannot do affects their motivation. When they have guidelines within which they can make decisions, they may be more likely to motivate themselves.

Below are examples of how an informal standard can be defined as a rule or a boundary:

Rule:

"All meetings will start on time regardless of the excuse.

Guideline:

"Meetings will start at the published time regardless of whether all attendees are present. Anyone showing up late will be responsible for coming up to speed without interfering with the meeting's progress."

This gives people the choice to show up late, understanding that choice has added responsibilities.

Rule:

"Yelling at or threatening another employee is inexcusable."

Guideline:

"People are expected to try to resolve issues they have with their co-workers before escalating the issue to their manager. The process of resolving issues must be done with respect for each other. If conflict becomes difficult to manage, the issue can be brought to a manager's attention. Employees are expected to use their best judgment."

By stating this standard in the form of a guideline, a manager provides the employee more control and discourages unnecessary escalation of trivial issues.

Rule:

"E-mail is to be used for necessary communication only."

Guideline:

"The e-mail system may not be used to communicate missed deadlines, critical customer issues, tardiness excuses, or anything that has a critical response time attached to it. Use your best judgment."

This better defines what is and isn't "necessary communication" but leaves room for employees to make their own decisions.

Rule:

"Employees must meet deadlines."

Guideline:

"If an employee determines he or she cannot meet a deadline, this must be communicated to the involved parties including managers as soon as the barrier to meeting the deadline is encountered. Use your best judgment."

Once again the employee has some control over the process.

Standards defined and communicated as guidelines give people some control over their lives. This makes the standard more effective in the end. People who feel they have some control over their environment are more likely to motivate themselves.

Effectiveness of Standards

The most critical element that impacts a standard's effectiveness is the manager's commitment to live within it. Whether managers like it or not, they become authority figures to the people they manage. With this increased authority goes the increased responsibility to set an example by living within the same guidelines as their people. Managers who violate a standard but continue to hold others accountable to that same standard are not being fair. This point must be considered when determining whether a standard is realistic. Managers who believe standards apply only to their people and not to themselves lose respect from employees. With the loss of respect goes a corresponding loss of influence of both the manager and the standard.

Arbitrary application of a standard also impacts its effectiveness. Managers who apply a standard when it is convenient or apply it selectively when they want to change a specific person's behavior impact the standard's effectiveness. They also impact their ability to manage. Evenhanded application of standards to both employees and managers greatly increases their effectiveness. Equitable application of standards strengthens accountability to them.

Setting and getting people to buy into expectations without controlling is more art than science. Employees are more likely to buy into an expectation if they believe it facilitates employee and company success and they have some control over the process of setting expectations.

Managers who control often avoid setting clear expectations or dictate the standards they think are important. A facilitative leader communicates and gets agreement upon realistic, measurable standards that are important to help the employee and company move forward. Managers who see themselves as superior to their employees will define informal standards as rules and regulations. Managers who see that their role is to help people become better decision makers will collaboratively set expectations as guidelines within which everyone is expected to operate.

Charles is violating a formal standard when he shows up late to work. He is violating an informal standard when he doesn't return voicemail messages or gives incomplete information so long as the standard has been communicated and agreed upon. The first step in turning Charles's performance around is to make sure he understands and buys into the formal and informal standards. A manager using an autocratic approach might simply tell Charles he must do things by the book, "or else."

Standards vs. Goals

Formal standards are the foundation laid by the organization to facilitate processes and protect people. Informal standards overlay formal standards and create an environment within which people can feel safe to make decisions. Without this foundation, goals can be demotivating. Without a safe base camp, it becomes difficult for people to push themselves to greater heights.

Managers who are good at goal setting but poor at clarifying standards often end up with employees who are reticent to accept challenging goals. When an employee has a difficult time determining whether he or she is doing a good job on a day-to-day basis, it is natural to be reticent to accept the increased responsibility of goals. Managers who are good at goal setting will often try to resolve a nonperformance issue by setting a goal for the employee to improve. This type of manager might try to "motivate" Charles to improve his punctuality by setting a goal for him to go one month without being late. Charles will accurately perceive this as an attempt to control.

Managers who have set a good foundation of standards have also set the stage for good goals.

Goals and Objectives

Goals stretch employees and are aligned with some company or departmental objective. A standard sets the guidelines within which goals are achieved. A goal is future based; a standard is process based. A goal is concerned with where the person, company, or department is going. A standard is concerned with how to get there.

The best goals have the same characteristics as standards; they are agreed upon, realistic, and measurable. But goals have one additional characteristic: a beginning and an end. They are future focused. The problem Charles had with his goal of introducing two new products to the market was caused by unclear standards, not poor goals.

Good goals always have standards attached to them. Charles's excuse for missing the product introduction because he didn't get the information on time from market research could have been prevented by setting a standard. The standard might be that employees must notify management in advance if they encounter a barrier to achieving a goal. Standards help clarify the process of reaching goals and help employees manage their own progress toward achieving goals.

Below are some examples of good goals that may be ineffective without standards:

Good goal:

"Improve average response time to customer inquiries from 8 hours to 6 hours by year-end." (Rational and may be realistic, but realize that implementation of this goal without a quality standard may result in quicker but poorer quality responses.)

Good goal:

"Implement plan to hold weekly meetings with Marketing department by end of first quarter." (Sounds good, but once again a quality standard will prevent weekly meetings that are unnecessary.)

It becomes obvious that a manager who is good at goal setting can still encounter problems when people achieve the goal but miss the point.

Operational and Developmental Goals

Goals or objectives also fall into two broad categories: operational and developmental. Operational goals are intended to improve business performance, efficiency, and effectiveness, to name a few areas. The idea behind operational objectives (remember that I use goals and objectives interchangeably) is that businesses must grow and become more effective to survive and thrive in the long term. Operational goals can apply to the business, like achieving a departmental metric or increasing revenue or profitability year to year, or they can apply to an individual or a team's performance metric. A customer service department may be expected to achieve a certain level of customer satisfaction and an individual member of that department might be expected to increase the number of customer calls per day to a certain number.

For purposes of this book and the underlying premise that it is focused on individual performance, I want to further explain the role operational and developmental goals play in the performance management process.

Individual Operational Objectives

In my career as a manager, I always insisted on a few operational objectives from each of my people. For me, I arrived at the number of operational goals after a lot of experience and trial and error, to be three. All my people had three and only three operational objectives, and developmental objectives. But only three of each with a total of six.

The number came from my experience attempting to help my team focus and being raised as a Catholic. For Catholics, everything happens in threes: Father, Son, and Holy Ghost; three days of Easter; and so on (a joke).

In my role as a former sales manager, there were always opportunities for salespeople to improve their documentation or make more sales calls per week or respond to more RFPs in a year. These are all operational objectives. And yes, salespeople always have a quota to achieve or overachieve. But those are always a given.

I looked for ways to make my folks more effective, efficient, and productive. Which meant that I had to pay attention to their shortcomings and struggles on the business side of the equation.

That was the easy part.

Developmental Objectives

The most challenging part of managing is the idea of developing your people. One issue is the wide variability in sophistication in a company's performance management process. While mature organizations, like Microsoft or Caterpillar, have a sophisticated and operationalized performance management system, many companies, even very large companies, leave it up to individual managers to use their own approach to people management and guidance. This is especially true in the sales part of many corporations; sales often get a pass when it comes to non-sales HR processes for some reason.

Like their operational goals, each of my people always had three developmental goals, three things they needed to improve upon, regardless of how much they met or exceeded expectations. For those who failed to meet expectations, their objectives were designed to get them back on track. For those on track, their objectives were designed to develop them for the next step in their career path, and for the overachievers, my challenge was to find things that challenged them to take things to the next level. Of course, this was all done in a collaborative and cooperative way. But all my people knew that they were expected to improve regardless of how they were currently performing.

Which is something I don't find that often in more casual or less-developed companies. When I ask managers about their developmental objectives for their people, they frequently make excuses about being very busy or managing people remotely so it is hard to develop and monitor progress. Once again, these are excuses, not reasons.

SMART Developmental Objectives

Many managers struggle with defining developmental objectives because they are difficult to define in ways that meet the criteria for SMART goals. However, when given enough thought and planning, it is almost always possible to follow the SMART criteria as well with a developmental objective as with an operational one.

The real issue is trying to create a developmental objective for an issue or a problem that is more of a standard than a goal. Standards should be communicated and enforced. Goals should be agreed upon and achieved. For instance, if I have a problem employee who constantly interrupts coworkers when they are especially busy, I don't want to create a developmental objective for this person to go a month without barging into people's offices and cubicles without regard for other's time and workload.

That would be lowering the bar for other's performance as well. I would communicate that this is inappropriate and not respectful of other's time and then convince the offender that it is in his or her best interest to be more respectful of other people's space as a proper "standard of conduct."

You can't set goals for people to "improve their attitude" or "be a team player" because these behaviors are standards expected of all employees. However, I often see objectives like these included in performance reviews and evaluations in major corporations and of high-level managers.

With enough thought, though, most behavioral and motivational issues can be broken down into actions that can be defined and communicated.

Let's look at a couple of goals that are better communicated and managed by being more clearly defined standards of behavior.

"Improve your attitude."

Regardless of how much a manager may want to correct a poor attitude, setting a goal for a person who shows negativity or morale issues is not the best way to make progress. When I ask a manager to explain how this person demonstrates a "poor attitude," I can always identify a behavioral and observable action that defines the usage of the term. Often a manager will say that this person complains about things but never does anything to try and improve the situation.

So the standard I would communicate is that everyone has the right to bring issues to management's attention. But when doing so, employees are expected to offer several possible solutions to the problem as well.

I once spoke to a manager who complained that one of his people lacked a "sense of urgency." When I delved into the issue further, it appears the employee rarely communicates where he is in the process of reaching a decision. Easily fixable with the standard that employees are expected to let managers know if they will miss a deadline "at the time they realize that they will miss the deadline and no later."

But creating true developmental objectives is a skill that can be acquired as well. There are always several areas that people can improve upon once you begin to give it some thought.

Areas I used to be particularly keen on developing people included presentation skills, leadership abilities (to prepare my people for management-level positions), communication skills, teamwork, decision-making abilities, business communication, and others. When faced with the more intangible abilities like leadership skills, managers get flummoxed at the notion of creating a developmental objective that fits the SMART criteria. But it isn't that difficult if you think more about process than result, once again.

Expectations and Facilitative Leadership

Expectations can be broken down into two areas: standards and goals. Each is a block in the process of building an environment in which people learn to self-manage. Without formal standards, informal standards become irrelevant. Without formal and informal standards, goals become demotivating.

When employees have a strong foundation of standards and well-written goals, they often motivate themselves. Facilitative leaders set guidelines that allow people to manage themselves. They get themselves out of the way and help people do their work. They facilitate employee motivation.

A manager's job is to help define the boundaries within which employees can achieve goals and grow. Failing to do so results in lost time due to corrective action or re-clarification of standards. The problem Charles has may be the result of unclear expectations. It is his manager's responsibility to clarify and get agreement before trying to hold him accountable.

Characteristics of Expectations Settings: Two Approaches

Autocratic Behaviorism	The Facilitative Leader
Emphasis on goals	Emphasis on standards
Sets standards as rules	Sets standards as guidelines
Uses goals to motivate	Creates environment for self-motivating
Dictates standards	Seeks consensus on expectations

CHAPTER 3

Feedback

There is no failure, only feedback.

—Robert Allen

The Six-Legged Sales Call

I often get the chance to work with sales managers in the field as they travel with their sales team. It is part of my consulting expertise, and my clients find it a good way to assess talent and help sales managers become better at developing their people.

On one such assignment, I was working with a sales manager and one of his reps in the biopharma industry. The salesperson was relatively new, and the sales manager was cotraveling as they often do in many industries to reduce the ramp-up time for new sales hires.

I had been asked to work with this sales manager because he was struggling with his people. His 360 feedback reviews indicated that his people did not feel he provided clear direction and developmental coaching. My standard method for determining the source of the issue is to sit with the manager and his or her salesperson while the manager conducts a pre-call discussion as I observe and take notes. Then I travel with both to the customer meeting (I am introduced as a consultant who is helping the company to improve their sales and leadership skills). After the customer meeting, I listen to the sales manager provide feedback and coaching the salesperson. This gives me a pretty good idea of how a manager can quickly increase his or her effectiveness and communication with the sales team. Most of the time, this works well and a manager's ratings improve significantly.

Not this time, however.

While the pre-call discussion went reasonably well, the customer meeting did not. It became quickly clear to me that this salesperson had a long way to go to become proficient at selling the company's product. Almost immediately, she lost control of the meeting as the customer diverged from the main discussion going off on a tangent about past customer service issues and the competition. Add to that the fact that several objections came up that were left unanswered. I was surprised that the sales manager let things go along these lines without jumping in to salvage the meeting and at least making some progress. As it was not my role, all I could do was watch.

I was very interested in how the post-meeting debrief was going to go after such a train-wreck of a meeting. We met in the cafeteria to debrief, which went like this.

The manager asked, "How did you think that meeting went?"

The salesperson responded, "Horrible, just horrible. I don't know why this keeps happening even when I prepare for these meetings. Things just seem to get offtrack and I end up accomplishing nothing."

To my surprise, the manager tried to make her feel better, "Don't be so hard on yourself. It wasn't as bad as you say it was. There was some good that came out of it."

"Really, like what?" she asked noticeably sarcastic.

"Well, I think you learned a valuable lesson in there. You learned that sometimes things don't go the way you want them to."

"Yes, but I don't feel I accomplished anything. What do I have to do to get better?" She asked frustrated.

"Just keep plugging away and keep doing what you are doing. Eventually it will start working for you."

"But what should I do differently?" What should I work on? How can I get better at my job?"

"Don't worry, don't worry. You're doing fine. Just keep up the good work and don't stop trying. You'll get it eventually. Don't be so hard on yourself."

I couldn't hold my tongue any longer; from this dialogue, I knew immediately what the problem was and wanted to send a strong message.

"Do you mind if I give some feedback to your rep?" I asked.

The manager turned to me with a kind of stunned look but gave me the okay.

I turned to the salesperson and looking her straight in the eye said, "You're right. That customer meeting was a train-wreck, wasn't it?"

A bit shocked but paying rapt attention, she responded, "Yes it was." And tears welled up in her eyes.

But I didn't back off. "And you're emotional not because you're sad, but because you're frustrated. Aren't you?"

"Yes," she replied, her eyes swelling even more.

"You're frustrated because you know that you are struggling but you don't know how to get any better. Is that right?"

"Yes," she said again, but this time with a dawning awareness.

And I said, "Well, that's a good place to start then. Let me explain why that meeting went so poorly and give you a couple skills that will help you avoid that happening in the future. Is that okay with you?"

"Yes," she said, her face brightening significantly.

Cheerleading Is Not Managing

Why is it that managers think that being a cheerleader is the same as being a manager? While managing, especially sales managing, does have some rah-rah aspect to it, cheerleading is not a skill. It is an attempt to motivate people through your own excitement. I remember sitting through motivational sessions when I was a middle manager in corporate America and thinking, "How does this help me do my job? Does this time I've taken out of my day help me make my objectives? Does this guy in front of the room understand the challenges of my job, or does he think that all anyone needs to be effective is to walk over some hot coals or zip from one tree to another while being encouraged to scream at the top of my lungs to release my inner demons?

Give me a break. And don't even *start* on trust falls . . .

Managing people takes all sorts of challenging skills like empathetic listening, detailed observation, and a keen understanding of human needs and desires. Sitting in a sweat-lodge with some pseudo-guru using amateur psychology to try and make you a better manager is, and I'm sorry to say this, stupid and a poor use of a manager's time and company money.

Feedback Rule #1: Be Honest and Constructive

If you treat people like adults, they often act like adults. When you treat them like children . . .

Adults can handle honest and sincere input on their performance especially if given by a manager that knows what he or she is doing. Soft-pedaling difficult feedback does not do justice to the employee. I am often asked by my clients to coach struggling employees and managers who are in jeopardy of losing their jobs or being blocked from promotion due to rather simple and easily corrected behaviors. Almost always, when I tell them that there is a problem, they are taken aback by the seriousness of the issue. Managers give mixed messages when they couch their communication in niceties and soft language to avoid making an employee uncomfortable. And that may be one indicator of a problem, the fact that the employee is too comfortable with the status quo. So perhaps you *want* to make them a bit uncomfortable. At least if it is a serious issue.

I have a bunch of friends that get together once a month for a dinner and movie, usually at my place. It is a regular thing with a regular crowd. But one of my friends, Tricia, has an annoying tendency to start a conversation often at the most suspenseful part in a movie. As I said, it is annoying but one of the things you put up with as a friend. One month I realized that Tricia was no longer invited to our movie night and inquired why. My friends said that they wanted to watch a movie without being interrupted for once, and so neglected to invite Tricia.

To me, this didn't seem fair. I invited Tricia despite my friend's advice telling them that I would handle it and make things good. As we watched the movie, as if on cue, Tricia asked if anyone was following the local elections. I interrupted her, "Hey Tricia. Do you mind if we talk about that after the movie is over?" "No problem," she replied and continued to watch in silence. Then again after about a half hour, she spoke up, "Did anyone see the Seahawks game this weekend? Great game, wasn't it?"

"Tricia," I said. "Can we please discuss the game after the movie?"

"Sure," she said looking a bit hurt.

After the movie, I had a chance to sit with Tricia and explain myself. I told her that when she talks through a movie, people have a problem concentrating and that it is a small but irritating behavior. In the end, she thanked me for bringing it up and letting her know about the issue. And she's fine now.

Which brings me to my point, which is that honest feedback can be incredibly helpful to people as long as you keep it constructive.

The best feedback, whether positive or negative (corrective), is always best when it is honest and constructive. Arm yourself with specifics before engaging with the employee and check your sources.

Like Tricia, one of the things Charles needs to do his job and meet his responsibilities is a clear understanding of the things he is doing well and the things he is not. So I asked him, "How often did your previous manager sit down with you and discuss your performance?"

"Well, that always happened once a year; at performance review time."

"Did you have any type of ongoing developmental plan?"

"What's that?"

"You know, a list of things that you do well and that you need to work on?"

"Never got anything like that from him. Only really met when he had a problem with me, when something was wrong."

"Do you know all the issues that he regarded as troublesome with you?'

"Well, he always seemed to scream about being late. But that's about it."

"Okay, Charles. I'm going to level with you. He had quite a few notes regarding your performance and I'd like to take them one by one and see if we can't get a handle on this and turn things around. Are you okay with that?"

"Um, okay. Not too sure but I'll give it a shot."

Pick Your Battles

Before you sit down with an employee, choose the specific behavior or behaviors you want to reinforce and limit your feedback to those specific behaviors. Managers tend to try and give as much feedback as possible when they have the attention of the employee. This can be overwhelming. A manager will be most effective by concentrating on one or two behaviors at a time. So, pick your battles. As a manager, you may want to communicate multiple areas of improvement, but remember that it is difficult for people to try and improve performance or behavior in too many areas. Stay with the 80/20 rule. Also, decide what you are going to say and how you are going to say it. As an example, let's say you recently sat through a presentation by one of your employees who did an excellent job of presenting an organized outline that was easy to follow. You will want to prepare to encourage the behavior of providing the outline.

Another aspect of encouragement is that it shows that you are paying attention. When it comes to Charles, I focused first on areas he did well to build his confidence and reinforce that my role is to help him begin to self-manage and motivate. That sends a positive message. At first, he was reluctant to see the value in our discussions and was suspicious of my motives. And I realized that it would take time to overcome some of his experiences with previous managers.

Feedback Rule #2: Get to the Point

For years I read and listened to a bunch of management consultants proselytizeon the best ways to give and receive feedback. And while I learned some good techniques, there were many that contradicted each other and some that just seemed stupid.

One idea I got from a management guru was to always start with a question when discussing performance. Actually, I had a boss who must have read that book because he used this particular technique regularly. He would stroll into my office, close the door, take a seat, and ask, "Hey Steve. How do you think you are doing in your job?" So first, by closing the door he set a tone that he had something to say he didn't want others to hear. Then by beginning with a question, he put it on me to figure out what he was getting at.

This always, always pissed me off. Why? Because I felt like, and often was, being set up. It was obvious that he came in with his own agenda. But because he had read this book, he thought that by getting me to open up and share my own shortcomings he was being a "compassionate" boss. It seemed like he was treating me like a child. If you have something to say, just say it. I'm a big boy. I can take it. And if I disagree with you, I will tell you. Sheesh.

Another stupid idea is what is called the "feedback sandwich." This is the technique in which your start with something good that the employee does, a skill or an approach or something. Then you follow it with the real reason you started the discussion, the behavior or performance you want the employee to change. And then you leave the employee with another area in which he or she is performing well. A feedback sandwich. Get it? Sometimes referred to as the "sh**" sandwich, for good reasons.

The only problem with this is that people are not dumb. They know you have an agenda and that the "sugar coating" is just sugar coating, an outside coating that hides the real reason for your interaction. One of the most important qualities that you want in your relationship with your people is credibility. And this type of feedback does not contribute to your credibility; it may detract from it.

So here is the deal. You only need to ensure that your feedback has two elements. All the feedback and coaching you provide to people need to be honest and constructive. That's it. Treat people like adults and they are more likely to act like ones. Treat them like children and you will encourage immature behavior.

In the initial meeting, Charles and I clarified and mutually agreed on a set of clearly defined expectations. The next step in helping Charles solve his performance problem was to provide him regular, frequent feedback on his progress. So we set up a weekly meeting to review progress and deliverables.

When asked how he received feedback from his previous manager, Charles said he received input mostly when he screwed up. His manager would point out what he was doing wrong and tell Charles how to fix the problem. He called it "constructive criticism."

Sometimes his manager would get frustrated and complain that Charles wasn't motivated. Charles insisted he was motivated but had his own way of doing things. Occasionally, when Charles did a good job, his manager would stop by his office telling him to "Keep up the good work!" which didn't help much.

Feedback Rule #3: It's Supposed to Be a Dialogue, Not a Monologue

Some managers like the sound of their own voice too much. They think that the definition of listening is waiting to talk. All feedback and coaching (and I use the terms interchangeably) should be an interactive and engaged dialogue with a give and take of ideas and opinions. Some managers tend to talk over their people while others don't give enough of their own input.

Introverted managers can have the same problems as overly-extroverted managers but for different reasons. A more reserved and introspective boss might seem disengaged and preoccupied when in fact they may be very engaged and paying close attention. People who work for these types of managers often feel like they are not being heard. Quick tip: if you are one of these types of managers, simply stating you own opinion can help. The phrase "Give me a minute to think about that" or "I'm not sure I agree with that" is a beginning in the right direction.

On the other side, overly extroverted managers could do well to stop themselves and ask questions, especially when they have a strong opinion. Asking an extroverted manager his or her opinion is like bait to a bass; sometimes they can't help themselves. And as a manager, you don't always want your people to know how you feel about every subject; at times, it is best to be hard to read. And if you always give your people the answer, they don't have to figure things out for themselves.

Try this as a practice; the next time one of your people ask you for your opinion, use the phrase "I have an opinion, but I'd like to hear yours first." You might learn something.

Engagement is about back-and-forth dialogue and challenge response. If you find yourself talking too much, then *be quiet*. And if you find yourself listening too much, state your opinion *out loud*.

Using questions, getting comfortable with silence, getting uncomfortable with silence, and listening to hear and not just validate your own opinion are keys to building an engaged environment in which people begin to feel comfortable self-managing and making decisions.

Reinforcing Feedback

The term "feedback" is in and of itself a neutral term. In the engineering world, a feedback loop is used to auto-calibrate and improve or extend performance. In that world at least, feedback is helpful whether it provides desired or undesired performance metrics. But in the corporate world, "feedback" often has a negative connotation, and for good reason. Many managers are less than adept at providing honest and constructive feedback to their people.

What comes to mind when you hear the words "Can I see you in my office?" Or "First, let me tell you that I think you're doing a great job . . ." See? Most people never want to hear these words because they know how the discussion is going to go.

So, let's start with the positive side of the feedback equation: discussion and dialogue to reinforce or extend good or above-average performance. While this often gets little attention, especially due to the results-driven nature of the corporate world, it is extremely important as a management tool. Catching people doing things right is a great way to build confidence and create self-managing behavior.

But I am often challenged with the question "Why should I praise people for just doing their job?" It is a legitimate point until you know the difference between praise and encouragement.

Be Specific and Behavioral

There is a big difference between praise and encouragement.

Managers who want to facilitate learning use encouragement to help people manage their own behavior. They realize employees are fallible and focus on the process of improvement, not accomplishment. When managers encourage, they concentrate on the process and progress toward the result. Managers facilitate achievement by identifying the end goal and managing the progress toward the result. Encouragement is part of a process-based management approach.

Encouragement shows employees that managers have respect and confidence in their ability to manage their own behavior. It recognizes effort and incremental improvement. Encouragement considers a person's imperfection and struggle to improve. And it is not dependent on achieving an result, only on effort. It can be applied in process.

Encouragement focuses on behavior and avoids value judgments. The process of using encouragement is participatory and requires managers pay attention and realize that the more they try to control, the more they might negatively impact a person's motivation.

Encouragement is a tool to help people manage their own progress. It helps managers to separate the individual from the act. Managers who use this type of feedback see employees as works-in-progress and respect the individual as having inherent self-worth independent of his or her behaviors. Encouragement focuses on people's improvement and their assets and strengths. Praise focuses on past performance.

The word "encouragement" comes from the Latin root "coure," meaning heart. The act of using encouragement is meant to help people have the heart or "courage" to make decisions for themselves, to self-manage. Managers who rely solely on praise usually see their people as sets of isolated behaviors engaged in achieving results for the manager or company. Good managers see their people as works-in-progress struggling to get better all the time. It is the manager's responsibility to help with this struggle.

There are situations where praise is appropriate. Praise can be a genuine expression of accomplishment and gratitude. Praise is best used to recognize significant progress or to celebrate large successes. The effective use of praise is based upon the underlying motivations of the manager and employee. If the manager's motivation is to control no matter how praise is delivered, the employee will feel controlled. If the employee is motivated by a need to "please" the manager, then she or he might become dependent on praise and use it in a subtle way to try and control the manager.

Discouragement?

Is discouragement the opposite of encouragement? While encouragement is an active process, discouragement can be the passive result of the process of encouragement. By encouraging certain positive behaviors, a person discourages negative ones. The difference might best be understood by determining the intended purpose of the feedback. If a person wants to reinforce a certain productive behavior, he or she will encourage that behavior. If a person wants to correct a negative behavior, he or she does so by encouraging the desired alternative positive behavior.

People who try to discourage behavior may be using the term to take the edge off "constructive criticism." Encouragement can be broken down into two different sets of steps depending on the manager's objectives in the encouragement process. There are two forms of feedback: one to reinforce positive behavior and another to correct negative behavior.

Charles's previous manager primarily used the praise approach to try and motivate Charles. Words like "great job" and "keep up the good work" are praise-words. They occur after the fact and refer to past behavior. They are specific only to the desired result.

And managers who pay primary attention to the bottom line and end results are usually good at praise. Praise to an employee who is not feeling good about his or her performance can further demotivate the employee. Overuse of praise demotivates because it feels as though the manager is not paying attention to the actual performance, only to outcomes. Employees who perceive their manager as authoritarian will see this type of feedback as a thinly veiled attempt to control. Praise is a tool that is part of an extrinsic motivation system based upon rewards and punishments.

The alternative to relying solely on praise is to use encouragement. Encouragement is process-based feedback. Using encouragement takes more time and thought, but the result is much more impactful on behavior. Managers who attempt to control behavior use praise. Encouragement helps people learn how to manage their own behavior. Using encouragement in place of praise or criticism facilitates the process of learning to make better decisions.

Elements of good, encouraging feedback include pointing out specific improvement areas or skills that are important to the job and help a person improve, not just achieve. So a manager has to pay attention to areas of needed improvement and think about how to reinforce those in a dialogue that is authentic and, well, encouraging.

Example of Praise:	"Great presentation, keep up the good work!"
Example of Encouragement:	"Great presentation. I especially thought you did a good job of handling all the questions and keeping everyone focused."
Example of Praise:	"You're doing really great!
Example of Encouragement:	"You are doing a really great job! Your attention to detail and keeping me in the loop are good skills. If I can help with anything let me know."

Using encouragement forces a manager to be more specific, more behavioral, and very much more helpful.

It isn't that the phrase "Great presentation!" or "You're doing great!" is bad; just incomplete. So, the next time you find yourself praising an employee, simply remember to finish the sentence.

Start Collaborative, but Be Ready to Become Directive

In my experience, one of the reasons managers avoid giving feedback is that some employees are very good at tying them in knots whenever they try to talk about performance. These are referred to as "rat holes," and an employee who is good at "rat holing" makes it difficult to send a clear message. You know the deal, you want to talk about an important issue, and before you know it, you have been dragged into a discussion on the failures of the corporate compensation program to satisfy this one employee's desires. A good indicator to a manager of whether he or she has a rat-hole problem is if he or she enters a discussion with an employee and the manager is the one who comes out with a "to-do" list.

All performance discussions should start off collaboratively. After all, it is a good practice to expect things to go well and have the employee accept responsibility for the issue or behavioral problem. But that is not always the case, especially with an employee who is adept at the skill of "rat holing." A key point to remember is that this irritating behavior is not about problem solving or improving situations. It is about power, and more specifically about the power the company has over employee expectations.

But regardless of the power issues, you might be asking yourself why I am bringing this up at this point, especially when discussing positive or reinforcing feedback and coaching. Well, some employees just always seem to have an axe to grind. And the person they want to grind their axe against is you, their manager. So while starting off with a cooperative approach is a good idea, realizing when the conversation begins to deteriorate is another key manager skill.

Here's an example of how things can get off track. Let's use the scenario that one of your people just completed a project that necessitated the input of multiple departments. Let's also say that this employee, we'll call her Chris, did a great job.

"Hey Chris. I saw you finished that project on time and with some great results."

"Yeah, well, no thanks to you or other departments. I had to do all the work myself without help from anyone!"

Now at this point, you might be thinking that an appropriate "collegial" response might be something like "Sorry to hear that Chris. Is there something I could have done to help you with that?" But if you know this person has a history of making conversations crazy, that is just inviting more drama.

A better response might be, "Sorry to hear that you had some challenges pulling it off. Well, all I wanted to say was that I think you did a great job of making sure everyone's input was recognized and integrated into the project. Thanks for that."

I call it the validate–redirect skill. You want to validate the employee's concern but redirect the conversation back to the issue at hand. Validating is recognizing the feelings of the person as legitimate; after all, we are all entitled to our opinions, even if they are based on false assumptions. But to keep the conversation productive, the manager has to control the direction of the dialogue. Your job is to be efficient, so it is important to pay attention to the direction the discussion is going, and take control to keep it on track.

When to Escalate?

I use the word "escalation" in this situation as a term for becoming increasingly directive in your conversation. As a manager, you should pick up on verbal and nonverbal signals as to whether the employee is taking responsibility for the issue at hand. And if there isn't any change in behavior, then perhaps another conversation is needed. If in the first coaching meeting, the employee seemed to accept responsibility and agreed to change the behavior but didn't, then it is time to escalate the discussion to a more direct and honest conversation. Remember, your goal is to have these conversations as seldom as possible. So, if you are not getting through to your employee, you have to become increasingly directive.

This is when the phrase "Can I see you in my office?" becomes appropriate. Or if the behavior continues after multiple conversations, think about the message you are sending. Once again, if you desire to avoid making the employee uncomfortable, you might want to revisit that; you might want to make this person realize that the comfort zone he or she has established is not in his or her best interest.

When I want to get on a person's radar about a specific multiple offense or just something egregious, I use phrases like "We need to talk" or "Something came up that we need to address immediately."

But keep in mind that your intention is not to punish, even if you may want to. Your intention is to help this person avoid the negative consequences of the behavior. Your intention is to help them, not punish them. So, making sure you are both on the same page as the discussion ends is crucial to this person's success.

A manager's job is to listen to his or her employees, but in this type of situation, no amount of listening is going to solve this problem. Remember where your control as a manager starts and ends. You cannot make someone like this happy, but you can reinforce and perhaps make a small positive impact on his or her performance.

One of the most important characteristic in an employee–supervisor relationship is trust. And while it is important, it is not always necessary. In fact, with some people, it's not even possible. New and young managers make the mistake of thinking that they must empathize with the person to prevent the discussion from getting heated or someone gets his or her feelings hurt. There are two sides to the trust equation. The first thing to do is to honestly ask yourself if you are trustworthy and whether you follow through and keep your promises. And if you are pretty sure that you have been fair, even-handed, and clear with an employee (especially over time), then trust should develop.

But the other side of the equation is the employee. Is this person capable of trusting a manager? It is important to realize that there will always be people who have authority issues, that regardless of how trustworthy and honest you are, they will not trust you because you are their boss. That doesn't mean you can't work with them, even for a lengthy period. But realizing that can save you a lot of time and energy trying to meet the trust expectations of an employee when they are unattainable.

So, from time to time, you may have to cut-off employees. Young and inexperienced managers tend to go down rat-holes until they learn how unproductive those discussions ultimately end up.

The wrong way to deal with this type of person is for the manager to avoid engaging at all costs. This doesn't work either. Why?

Frame the Discussion

Because many people, like Charles, naturally become defensive when their manager approaches, it is important to set the tone of the interaction before encouraging. Using the example above, a manager might set the tone by stating, "I *thought the presentation went really well.*" This sets the tone in a positive way and sends the initial message that this interaction will be positive and people will be more open to encouragement when a positive tone is set. Praise has a place in encouragement, and like I said, all you need do as a manager is finish the thought.

You want to communicate from the start, that this interaction is going to be positive and that you are happy with the performance or behavior. This isn't the same as "couching" or softening the message because the message is positive. Most people won't argue with you when you are encouraging positive performance.

Get Specific

To increase the retention of the positive behavior, emphasize the key skill or skills by specifically pointing out not only the positive behavior but also the impact that behavior has on the issue at hand. Instead of saying, "*You did a good job of providing an outline,*" a manager makes the interaction that much more impactful by adding, "*You did a particularly good job of organizing and presenting an ordered outline. I think this helped people follow you better and increased the effectiveness of your presentation.*"

This second statement is more specific and shows the manager is paying attention to process and the results. A manager may want to end this encouragement with a question such as "What do you think?"

But it is critical not to let the employee turn the interaction into a discussion about what he or she could do to improve. Mixing the positive message with needs for improvement will lessen the impact of the encouragement. If possible, it is better to separate encouragement from criticism except for Type A personalities. People with a driven style may feel as though the conversation has been left unfinished and strange without something to improve upon. But be careful; some employees might take the interaction as mostly negative if you add anything corrective as well. So, read the situation and the person and make a judgment call.

End on the Positive

Realize that mixing negative and positive feedback invalidates the positive and lessens the impact of the negative. If a manager's intention is to correct negative behavior, he or she can include some positives after the problem-solving step, but spike the main message of the behavior to correct. If a manager wants to reinforce positive behavior, including any negative behavior will often overshadow and wipe out the desired reinforcement.

I like to close the conversation with a positive and specific message that encourages the person to continue to self-assess and manage his or her own development. One of my favorite statements is something like, "You know, when I see you taking things like this on, it gives me a lot of confidence in your abilities."

I surmise from his file that this is what most likely happened with Charles. There was very little documentation about either formal or informal discussions between the two of them. And after working with Charles, I realized that he can be difficult. But when I became direct, honest, and constructive, he would eventually back off and listen. But this took time and much self-reflection to figure out the shortcomings I bring to interactions as well.

Even trying to provide encouragement and reinforcement to an employee like this can be a challenge. The notes in Charles's personnel file indicated that Charles was unmotivated and unresponsive to either praise or criticism. To correct the situation, Charles was given a goal to attend two seminars: one to improve interpersonal skills and one to improve time management. Once again, while the seminars may be a good idea developmentally, I said to myself that his manager was averse to confronting and dealing with challenging people. Charles's overall opinion was that the main purpose of his manager's feedback was to get him to fall in line. He complained that his manager spent more time correcting him after the mistake than trying to help him understand how to prevent it.

Charles and his manager were frustrated because the feedback used in their interactions was primarily results based: praise for a job well done and criticism for one done poorly. Both praise and criticism are forms of results-based feedback.

Constructive Feedback

Criticism is another attempt to control behavior through a system of rewards and punishments. Constructive feedback, however, is important and timely input into a professional's performance and behavior. I hear the term "constructive criticism" all the time, and mostly it is well intentioned. But if a manager's objective is to create a safe environment for his or her team, it is important to take into consideration a couple of important points.

Praise in Public, Correct in Private

This seems like a no-brainer, but for some reason I hear all the time about managers chewing out employees in front of others. Public shaming does motivate people; it motivates people to avoid their manager. There is no good reason for a manager to criticize another person in front of his or her peers. It's a stupid way to correct and reduces the credibility more of the manager than of the offender. Regardless of what you may have heard, dressing someone down in front of others is not a good management strategy. It will always be seen as controlling because it is.

Get to the Point

When I ask people how they would like to receive corrective feedback, they almost always say, "Get to the point but be gentle!" Dragging out the discussion or using questions to get the employee to open up can be perceived as duplicitous and controlling. Being straightforward, especially when correcting, sends a clear message.

It is possible to be both cooperative and assertive with an employee. Some managers think these two qualities are mutually exclusive. Even if you need to deliver an especially strong message, you don't need to be a jerk. And getting to the point is not the same as being a jerk. Quite a few people who worked for me felt I had a hidden agenda whenever I had a discussion with them regarding problematic behavior or performance, until they "got it." "It" being that I always, always had their best interests in mind. One way I communicated my intentions was by being straightforward and avoiding "fluff" when engaging with them on challenges. My most used line was "Got a minute?" And while at first, this made people a bit uncomfortable, they all eventually got used to "the drill," as I called it.

Send a Clear Message

If an issue is important enough to warrant a corrective discussion, then it is important enough to want to avoid further discussions. I am often asked how many times a manager should have to address an issue with an employee before documenting the issue or even issuing a verbal or written warning. When I dig into these individual situations, it becomes clear very quickly that in previous performance discussions, the employee did not leave with a clear sense of how important it was to change the behavior.

The more important the issue, the less you want to revisit it. And the key to achieving that end is making sure the employee knows how important it is to change. Mixed messages and "couching" your message with softer words does not help in achieving the desired results.

And the *best* way to ensure buy-in to altering behavior is if the employee understands that it is in their best interest to do so. So, part of a manager's job is to persuade and convince the person that the current behavior/performance issue does not contribute to their success in this company or as a person.

As a manager, whether you like it or not, you have authority. The two things you get when you are put in charge of a group are authority and responsibility. I would argue that you get more responsibility than authority, but that discussion could take longer than this book has pages for.

But in business, a manager makes an evaluation of a behavior and provides the employee with feedback. The evaluation is done extrinsically or outside of the employee, and he or she is the recipient of the praise or criticism. This type of feedback is "done" to the employee.

Because this type of feedback is "done" by a manager to an employee, it makes that manager responsible for the behavior and the manager has to "manage" it. It produces compliance, but rarely commitment. Praise and criticism are attempts to motivate through external evaluation and social control. They reinforce the employees' belief that success is dependent upon their manager's evaluation, not their own. In a management environment that depends mostly on praise and criticism, employees usually perform well if their manager keeps up the praise. They often become demotivated in the process of receiving criticism. These approaches build management-dependent behavior, like Alex at the beach.

Managers who rely on praise and criticism may believe they are managing the progress of the individual, when in fact they are trying to manage results. This type of feedback is easy to do because managers need only pay attention to the result, not the process. Therefore, it takes less time and energy. What managers eventually get from using this type of feedback are employees that are dependent on their manager to determine their success. Using praise and criticism can develop more dependency. Once again, this is reinforced by the "just do it" management culture.

You Can Treat One Employee Differently from Another

Well, here is another management guideline you may not be aware of but it is true. As a manager, you can treat one employee different from another . . . you can. When I say this to managers, I often get raised eyebrows. That response, I think, is mostly due to being told and taught that everyone must be treated the exact same way, especially in the corporate environment. Repeatedly Human Resources has warned about the dangers of sexism, racism, ageism, or whatever other population qualification that is not only unfair but exposes the company to legal liability.

But here is something I rarely hear any HR department explain.

A manager *can* treat his or her employee differently due to a performance issue under one circumstance; That this employee knows he or she is being treated differently because of a performance issue. If a manager begins to treat an employee differently without explaining the reason, it is normal for a person to begin to think that he or she is being treated differently because of . . . insert your protected group here.

So if you begin to avoid having any conversations with someone like Charles, and he notices this, he may begin to think that you are treating him differently because in this case, perhaps he is a member of a sometimes disenfranchised group. Once you let a person know that he or she is struggling with an issue, you can then begin monitoring his or her performance in this area. You can meet more often with him or her than you do with your other people. But you must *let them know*!

Constructive Feedback Process

The process for having an effective and productive corrective discussion starts off faster, but more time is required at the back end with the addition of a problem-solving step. And there is a preparation step that is crucial.

Choose

A person can only focus on improving one or two challenges at any one time. Using the same presentation example, let's say a manager had previously clarified the expectation that all presentations must start with an overview of the purpose and agenda for the benefit of the attendees. This manager just finished sitting in on an employee's presentation in which no agenda and purpose were covered. Prior to setting the tone, the manager must choose whether to reinforce something the employee did well or correct the negative behavior. Once the manager has decided to correct the negative behavior, he or she must choose how to set the tone, emphasize, and problem solve. The preparation step when correcting negative behavior is more critical than when encouraging positive behavior.

Set Tone

Most people want bad news quickly without beating around the bush. This manager might start out by saying, "*Something concerned me about the presentation.*" This helps prepare the employee for the next point. If your intention is to truly address inappropriate behavior or lack of performance, then letting the employee know this upfront is a fair and reasonable approach.

Emphasize

At this point the manager must be firm and matter-of-fact. The specific behavior and its impact must be delivered with as little personal judgment as possible. If you as a manager have checked your sources (if you were not there to directly observe the situation), then being honest, constructive, and to the point will serve you well.

> *"The presentation started out without a purpose and agenda. This limited the presentation effectiveness."*

Problem Solve

At this point the manager should avoid excuses. If the expectation was realistic (which in this situation it surely is), measurable, and agreed upon, then the manager can validate without accepting. For example, if the employee says he or she was too busy, the manager might reply, "*I know we are all very busy, but we all agreed to start our presentations this way.*" Then proceed to a problem-solving step by saying, "*How can you (or we) prevent this from happening in future presentations?*"

It is imperative that the manager is careful to keep himself or herself out of the equation. Instead of saying, "I don't like the presentation starting that way," the manager will be clearer by saying, "*The expectation we agreed upon was . . . .*" The more collaboratively a manager sets standards, the easier it is to keep himself or herself out of the way.

Remember to Pick Your Battles

Before you sit down with an employee, choose the specific behavior or behaviors you want to reinforce and limit your feedback to those specific behaviors. Managers tend to try and give as much feedback as possible when they have the attention of the employee. This can be overwhelming.

A manager will be most effective by concentrating on one or two behaviors at a time. So, pick your battles. As a manager, you may want to communicate multiple areas of improvement, but remember that it is difficult for people to try and improve performance or behavior in too many areas. Stay with the 80/20 rule. Also, decide what you are going to say and how you are going to say it. As an example, let's say you recently sat through a presentation by one of your employees who did an excellent job of presenting an organized outline that was easy to follow. You will want to prepare to encourage the behavior of providing the outline.

When it comes to Charles, I focused first on areas he did well to build his confidence and reinforce that my role is to help him begin to self-manage and motivate. Another aspect of encouragement is that it shows that you are paying attention. That in itself sends a positive message. At first, he was reluctant to see the value in our discussions and was suspicious of my motives. But I realized that it would take time to overcome some of his experiences with previous managers.

Below are additional examples of autocratic feedback and encouragement using Charles's performance challenges.

Situation

Charles completes a lengthy report within a specific time frame and meets all standards.

Praise

Great job, Charles. Keep up the good work.

Encouragement to Reinforce Positive Behavior

Thanks for getting the report done on time, Charles. That really helps our organization's reputation with the departments we depend on.

Situation

Charles doesn't get the job in on time but meets the standards.

Praise with Criticism

Hey, Charles, nice job on the report. Next time make sure you get it to me on time.

Encouragement with Constructive Feedback

Charles, the report you submitted looks great. We will get even more leverage with other departments if we can deliver these sorts of things in the time frame we agree to. Thanks for your efforts on this.

Feedback Is a Developmental Discussion; Not an Accountability Discussion

Feedback and accountability are related but not the same thing. In fact, it is imperative to keep these two very important discussions separate and distinct. Feedback is coaching and engagement to help an employee understand how important it is to change behavior or increase productivity; it is about encouraging an employee to either continue to extend positive performance or to discourage unproductive behaviors. Accountability is about consequences and the last step in the facilitative leadership process. Accountability is using results or lack thereof as a last resort to change behavior.

So if your intention is to provide feedback, then you need to stick with feedback.

But without a clear distinction of when a manager has moved from feedback to accountability it is difficult to tell. So here is the rule I use to distinguish between the two; you have moved to accountability when you reveal the potential consequences of continued misbehavior or performance.

The best example for understanding this is that of a parent correcting a child's behavior. It is always best to do it without threats (not that presenting an employee with a potential consequence is a threat, but more on that in the next chapter). As a parent, once you threaten time-out (consequence), you have essentially moved to accountability. That is, of course, unless you make idle threats to your kids all the time. In which case, I'm sure you have your parenting challenges as well.

The line between feedback and accountability is using the threat of discipline or punishment as a tool to get people to fall in line. That is, because once you communicate a consequence, you must follow through. For that reason, it is crucial to your credibility that you keep that card in your pocket until you have no other choice but to use it. By focusing on clear expectations and regular honest and constructive feedback it is possible to avoid accountability discussions altogether.

This is not easy, especially when you are frustrated and angry with a person's behavior or performance. Letting the behavior get to you and lashing out is a normal human response to continued mistakes, but it does not help you as a leader. You should control your emotions, stay objective, and focus on the individual and his or her progress.

Feedback and the Facilitative Leader

Feedback can be delivered in two ways. Praise and criticism have a place, but are seen by employees as attempts to control. Encouragement focuses on the process of meeting expectations and achieving goals. Employees see an encouragement approach as one of collaboration and mutual respect.

Facilitative leaders recognize and encourage progress and improvement. They don't see people as sets of behaviors. Rather they see them as works-in-progress. A manager who focuses exclusively on the result is not managing; he or she is avoiding the hard work of engaging and working with his or her people. A hallmark of an autocratic-behaviorist approach is an overreliance on praise and criticism to manage behavior. Employees see this as controlling and demanding obedience.

If managers see that their primary job is to hold people accountable for reaching objectives, they will see people either as achieving or as not achieving. The facilitative leader's job is to help people become more responsible. He or she does so through building trust and confidence by helping employees see the incremental improvements in their abilities. Managers that neglect to give frequent feedback or rely solely on giving praise and criticism are not managing, and they may be interfering with their people's progress.

To use encouragement properly, managers must pay attention to people's behaviors and progress as well as the bottom line. Using this approach helps managers to build their employees' confidence. The goal of a manager is to develop employees' self-management skills and to help people become responsible decision makers.

Managers owe and are owed frequent feedback. Those who rely on praise and criticism are not managing people; they are trying to manage results. It is unfair when managers withhold feedback but expect good performance.

Charles's second problem stems from his manager's attempt to "motivate" him to achieve results. I worked closely with Charles, providing him regular and honest input into his decisions and judgment calls. We set up a weekly meeting to review deliverables and discuss his progress in the areas he struggled. Slowly, ever so slowly, we established a good working relationship. The key to this was Charles understanding my intentions. I was sincerely focused on salvaging Charles's standings in the company and his career. And my intentions were communicated much more effectively by my actions than by my words. I began giving him the benefit of the doubt and soon changed our weekly meetings to bimonthly.

He started showing up on time to meetings, which I noticed; I showed appreciation for his attempts to be more punctual. He also began asking me for help on some of the projects he fell behind on and, more importantly, began to trust me enough to relate when he felt as though he might miss a deadline; he often communicated it earlier than necessary, but that was a minor irritation.

I was beginning to think that Charles might make it after all.

CHAPTER 4

Accountability

What you allow, is what will continue.

—Unknown

There are many misconceptions about the term "accountability" in the corporate world. As I mentioned before, most employees define it in corrective or disciplinary terms, when it is not. The term has a much broader and useful meaning than the narrow definition many equate with it.

And as I stated earlier, accountability is about consequences, consequences for poor performance or behavior as well as for good performance or desired behaviors.

So for me, the question was whether or not Charles experienced the consequences of his behavior?

Now that Charles and I have agreed on a set of clear expectations and I've been providing him regular, honest, and constructive feedback, what do I do if he continues to fall back into his old patterns of nonperformance? His previous manager avoided dealing with Charles's problems until they impacted other employees' performance and could not be avoided. When forced to confront Charles, he threatened disciplinary action or shifted Charles's responsibilities so he would have less impact on others. This left himself and Charles's peers in the difficult position of having to pick up the slack for Charles. When Charles did respond well and perform, he received praise and was sometimes rewarded with a little time off.

In our discussion about his tardiness at meetings, Charles shared that his manager always complained about this but took no action. After many attempts to change this behavior, Charles was reprimanded. His manager complained how frustrating it was that Charles knew what was expected but continued his poor behavior.

When Charles showed up on time, his manager made a point of reinforcing this behavior by thanking him. Charles responded well for a short while, but after time slipped back into his old behavior of showing up late. His previous manager's attempts to hold him accountable had little long-term effect on Charles's behavior. Charles eventually did whatever he wanted and came to expect a reward for performing and became apathetic when faced with punishment. In despair his manager documented the behavior in Charles's personnel file. Finally, Charles's manager avoided dealing with the problem by transferring him to another department; mine.

Charles's previous manager was frustrated mainly because Charles did not respond to attempts to hold him accountable through reward and punishment. Rewards and punishments are tools used by managers to control. This approach works in a system when the person in power is assumed to have the right answer; it demotivates when people have choices. Rewards and punishments are seen by employees as attempts to make them conform to the rules. Their reaction is often resistance or grudging compliance. Rarely is it motivation.

Accountability and Responsibility

Using a system of rewards and punishments does not necessarily make people more accountable; it can make them less. Managers who use reward and punishment systems mistakenly assume that by holding people accountable they can make them more responsible. No person can make another responsible. Responsibility is something that is accepted or rejected. Managers often try to give responsibility to people who don't want to take responsibility. But there are many situations in which a person is given responsibility, but refuses to accept it.

The alternative to trying to make people responsible is to help people begin to hold themselves accountable for their own performance.

Let's define some terms here. Responsibility is the degree to which a person or group is accountable for the consequences of their decisions. In fact, accountability is accepting the consequences for performance or behaviors. People can be held accountable, or they can hold themselves accountable, or both. Taking responsibility is an internal decision people make to hold themselves accountable for the consequences of their actions. Before people will take responsibility, they must have confidence in their ability to take a good course of action.

The logical connection managers make is that they can make people more responsible by holding them more accountable. That is control. People take responsibility when they choose to hold themselves accountable. That is self-management.

A person chooses to become more responsible by independently accepting the accountability. The degree to which a person holds himself or herself accountable defines the degree to which they feel responsible. Facilitative leaders create opportunities for people to accept responsibility; they teach them how to be accountable.

How does a manager facilitate accountability? People will accept accountability and take responsibility if they have some control over and confidence in the choices they make. When people have no input into what they will be held responsible for, they naturally avoid being held accountable, especially if the expectations are unreasonably high or unattainable. That is why it is so important to have a mutually agreed-upon set of objectives and a reasonable code of conduct.

I remember when a man named Paul Lopez took over as CEO of Ford Motor Company in the 1980s. He was a financial guy with a peculiar approach to managing his people. First, he insisted that his people wear their watch on the dominant arm, lefties on the left hand and righties on the right hand. He said that this was to keep people "hyper-vigilante" in cutting costs. He also insisted that everyone have only coffee and a banana for breakfast to stimulate morning work productivity.

Once in charge, he tore up all the existing vendor contracts and demanded that all suppliers lower their prices by 20 percent, to begin with. And despite very good support from the Board, his people sabotaged his efforts and nearly brought Ford to a standstill. Lopez's eccentric and authoritarian leadership style almost bankrupted the company and resulted in a long-lasting drain of capital and human resources. For all his talk, it most likely never occurred to him that he couldn't make his people responsible for unfair and unrealistic expectations.

Only when people feel they have some control and are confident in their ability to make good decisions will they accept responsibility. This makes sense for anyone who has worked for an autocratic leader. Only when people feel empowered will they choose to hold themselves accountable and self-manage. People become more responsible as they begin to hold themselves accountable for the consequences of their decisions.

My first step in helping Charles begin to take responsibility was by reaching agreement on a set of clearly defined expectations. The list of goals and behavioral expectations we co-developed and negotiated established a foundation of accountability. But it didn't stop there. Then, using honest and constructive feedback, over time he developed confidence in his ability to achieve the objectives and to live within the behavioral standards of the company. The key point was that I had to do this with him, not to him.

Holding people accountable builds management-dependent behavior because the locus of control is outside the individual. For example, a parent who tries to control will put a glass of juice in front of a child and tell him or her, "Don't spill it." When the child spills the juice the parent yells at the child telling him or her, "If you do that again I'm going to send you to bed without dinner." This is an example of using reward and punishment to hold the child accountable. The child quickly learns to depend on the parent to determine what a good choice is and what a bad choice is. The behaviors become parent dependent. The locus of control is outside of or extrinsic to the child. The child doesn't learn to hold himself or herself accountable.

On the other hand, another parent might clarify the expectation by telling the child that if the juice is spilt, then he or she must clean it up and refill the glass. When the child spills the juice, he or she experiences the direct consequences of the actions. The child makes the decision based upon the consequences of the behavior, not the consequences delivered by the parent. The child will learn to monitor and manage his or her own behavior. The parent who is holding his or her child "accountable" spends more time "parenting" or controlling short-term behavior.

(Let me say at this point that managing people's performance is not the same as parenting; it's more like babysitting☺. That's a joke.)

Managers who use reward and punishment as consequences, like parents who try to control, inhibit the ability of an employee to take responsibility. Trying to get an employee to make better decisions through accountability makes him or her dependent on the manager to define what is or is not a good decision. Good managers facilitate the opportunities for employees to experience the direct consequences of their decisions. They facilitate opportunities to learn.

Positive Accountability: Intrinsic or Extrinsic Motivation

I work with many managers who feel that their job is to get their people "pumped up." Especially in sales, managers get quickly frustrated with an employee who doesn't share the same enthusiasm as he or she does. There are a couple of statements managers make that point directly to this issue. "She doesn't have a sense of urgency" or "He gets too far into the weeds and slows us down." These statements are unfair and usually said by a manager who believes that everyone should have the same sense of devotion and excitement about the job.

To debunk just these two specific examples, a person who takes his or her time to make decision does not necessarily lack a sense of urgency; perhaps some situations require more caution than others. And as for getting "too far into the weeds," there are some people who desire more information before making decisions than you do. If you provide more detail than is your style, you might see quicker decision making.

The point here is that human motivation is much more complex than something that might positively respond to cheerleading.

From a higher and perhaps more informed position, a manger should understand that, in fact, there are two different types of motivations that influence behavior: intrinsic and extrinsic.

Some people are more heavily influenced by internal, more personal, and more deeply rooted motivating factors. Again, you can look at Marlow's Hierarchy of Need pyramid, but when it comes down to individuals, things like being part of a team, doing interesting work, and nonbusiness interests like charity and family, all impact a person's desire and ability to do a job. Both Eddie Bauer and R.E.I. pay employees for charity work and helping to clean up the outdoors. And so these companies attract people with those same values.

On the other side are more people driven by extrinsic factors, those that come from outside the person.

The main extrinsic motivators used in the American business culture are rewards and punishments. Extrinsic rewards can take many forms, such as money, recognition, and praise. Examples of punishments are criticism, withholding rewards, and reprimand. At a company like Oracle, one of the main incentives is to be promoted and earn higher and higher incomes. And the culture reflects that. From my work at Oracle, it is clear that conflict is encouraged, business performance is rewarded, and those who deliver results get to the next level. Is that wrong? No, just different. But I rarely run into an ex-R.E.I. or ex–Eddie Bauer person working at Oracle.

Extrinsic motivators come from someone or some organization extrinsic to or outside of the person. Because they are things "done to" the person, extrinsic motivators are used to control people's behavior. The underlying premise is that if you do what the manager or company wants, then you get rewarded; if you don't, you don't.

Extrinsic motivators have an upside and a downside. In an industry like enterprise software, with rapidly changing market conditions, intense competition, and a more Darwinian environment, perhaps a company that emphasizes extrinsic reward systems has the right idea. For other industries, and I must say other personality types, an overemphasis on rewards and discipline might be too much.

But the downside of the overemphasis in extrinsic motivating factors like money, promotion, recognition, and so on is an environment that has ever-escalating demands on people's time, energy, and life.

They do motivate people to do what others want them to do. But they are self-reinforcing, unlike intrinsic motivators. Like Alfie Cohen said in his breakthrough book *Punished By Rewards,* "[T]he problem with the overuse of extrinsic reward systems is that they do motivate . . . but they mostly motivate people to strive for more rewards."

They build dependent behavior because the person being "motivated" depends on the person delivering the extrinsic motivator to determine whether he or she has behaved in the desired way. Managers who rely too heavily on extrinsic motivators build management-dependent behavior.

Intrinsic motivators are internally defined by a person. They self-motivate. Intrinsic motivators are things a person finds interesting and likes to do. They are done for their own sake, not for someone else's. They can be an individual's sense of achievement and improvement or the desire to learn or be part of a group.

Intrinsic motivators are not controlled by outside forces; people motivate themselves. Intrinsic motivators become stronger in environments in which people have more control over their choices. They weaken when people feel controlled. Extrinsic motivators become stronger the more they are used because people come to expect them.

The overreliance on extrinsic motivators is a symptom of an autocratic-behaviorist management approach. Managers who rely on extrinsic motivators to control behavior usually end up with people who rely on managers to provide extrinsic motivators. By focusing on the result, managers create an environment in which their people focus on the end result: the reward. Thus, managers create management-dependent behavior and an ever-higher spiraling demand for extrinsic rewards.

I often see this difference manifested when comparing American and European companies. Employee tenure is, in general, much longer in European companies than it is in American companies. You can think of this in terms of loyalty or independence or as a function of the two different reward systems. In many American companies, money and title define success. This is not as much the case in Europe. European employees are more driven by intrinsic rewards like being part of an organization, having significant time off to spend with family, and a less-competitive quality of life. And I think it is fair to say that the individualistic and competitive culture in the States is less attractive to European workers, in general.

The Responsibility Continuum

Many managers make quick judgments that their people are either responsible or irresponsible. For some reason, people get pigeon-holed into being accountable for their actions or not. This is not very fair and is another effect of our "just do it" culture. To let go of control, it is important to realize that people are more complex than a single "modifier." I have many people in my life, including my children (and myself, I must admit), that are responsible and accountable in many areas but who struggle to be responsible in others.

Less Responsible	More Responsible
Given responsibility	Take responsibility
Make poor decisions	Make good decisions
Held accountable	Hold themselves accountable
Management dependent	Self-management behavior
Narrow guidelines	Broad guidelines

The key to moving past this type of thinking is to realize that all employees are works-in-progress.

The facilitative leader sees people as works-in-progress along the responsibility continuum.

Using Accountability to Correct Behavior

The goal of a facilitative leader is to help a person move from less responsible to more responsible, to help employees hold themselves accountable. When a person is in the process of developing a sense of responsibility, it is necessary for a manager to define narrower guidelines for making choices to ensure business progress. People who are more responsible can make more choices because they and their managers have more faith in their ability to make good decisions. A person who is further along on the Responsibility Continuum can have broader guidelines within which he or she can make decisions.

The three tools facilitative leaders have at their disposal to help people become more responsible are feedback, strategic nonintervention, and choice of consequences. The underlying groundwork that supports these tools is clear expectations and honest and constructive feedback. These tools, along with clear expectations, help employees to move along the responsibility continuum.

Feedback Revisited

Feedback in the form of encouragement helps people move along the Responsibility Continuum. Praise and criticism focus on achievement and non-achievement after the fact. Encouragement focuses on progress and future improvement. By design, encouragement helps people become more confident in their ability to make choices and take responsibility.

The purpose of encouragement is to build courage. When managers use encouragement, they are automatically helping people to make better choices. A manager using praise and criticism may be preventing people from learning how to make their own decisions.

Strategic Nonintervention

Another tool managers have for facilitating learning is the concept I call "strategic nonintervention," defined as letting people experience the direct consequences of their decisions, good or bad, within reasonable limits. People learn best when they experience direct consequences. When a person touches a hot stove, he or she experiences the burning sensation and makes the decision never to do that again. When a child spills milk and has to clean it up and refill the glass, this is the use of direct consequences. Sending them to bed has no logical connection to the spilt milk, so the child does not learn to take responsibility for his or her actions.

Strategic nonintervention lets people experience the direct consequences of their choices.

But strategic nonintervention is just that: strategic. Returning to the analogy of a parent trying to teach a child to ride a bike, the parent may let the child practice in a school yard but not in the street. This is a strategic decision based on the possible consequences. Once the child learns to ride safely in the school yard, then he or she can move to the street. For Charles, since he had a poor history of decision making, I gave him a short leash, so to speak. But as he developed better and better judgment, I slowly allowed him more room and opportunities to use his own judgment.

But I had to take into consideration a couple of things before stepping out of his way and letting his "failure" become a learning process for him.

In order to ensure that the opportunity to learn occurs in a manner that is in the best interest of the employee and the company, the facilitative leader has to evaluate three different criteria before using strategic nonintervention, as I did with Charles.

The criteria that a manager must use to determine whether to let employees experience the direct consequences of their decisions are as follows:

Ability: What are the chances of the employee making a poor decision?

It is the manager's responsibility to match tasks with ability. If the employee has little experience with the task, strategic nonintervention may be inappropriate in this situation. While there is something to be said about getting out of the way of learning, it is important for a manager to realize that another one of his or her responsibilities is to protect employees from their own poor choices.

I recently worked with a manager who thought it was his responsibility to get his people promoted. And to some extent it is and can be a measure of a manager's leadership abilities, developing people into leadership positions. But in this manager's case, he was not considering the needs and abilities of his people in the equation. He has a history of recommending his people for promotions when they were not nearly ready for the responsibility. This put some of his people into situations that were not in their best career interests. A manager's role is to develop people but also manage their expectations regarding advancement and development.

Impact on employee: Will the failure in this situation significantly impact the employee's confidence?

Another important consideration is how damaging a poor decision would be to the confidence and willingness to act on their own of the employee. If the employee makes a poor decision, will the direct consequences of that decision inhibit his or her willingness to make future decisions? It is the manager's responsibility to evaluate the impact on the employee. A manager must evaluate whether the consequences of making a poor decision will negatively impact the willingness of the employee to make future decisions and inhibit his or her growth. Creating an environment that is safe for people to take chances and self-manage takes a bit of thought and reflection. Keeping in mind that your people are works-in-progress and making mistakes is part of learning puts managers into a developmental mindset when guiding his or her people's career.

Impact on the business: Will failure seriously threaten the success of the organization?

Coming back to the ocean liner analogy, if a poor decision will sink the ship, perhaps this is not a good situation to put your organization in. I work with United Healthcare hospital contractors, who are able to negotiate reimbursement contracts that are in the tens of millions of dollars. They often complain that their management puts them in uncomfortable positions because they do not have the authority to walk away from a hospital or hospital group if the contract does not meet their objectives. This is a decision that is reserved for upper levels of management to make alone. I always ask them if they would want to be in that position, especially with the impact not only on United's revenue growth goals, let alone the future career of the contractor who makes the wrong decision.

So, the question is, will the learning that occurs from that decision outweigh the short-term loss in productivity?

It is the manager's responsibility to weigh the organizational impact of a poor decision against the learning that might occur for the employee. If the employee learns a valuable lesson but the department misses a crucial deadline, then the learning point might be lost.

Let's use a simple example of Charles's tardiness at meetings. In this situation, his previous manager got frustrated with him and threatened punishment. Although he rarely followed through, it appears making idle threats were one of his main managing tools (or I should say weapons).

Evaluating these three criteria to determine whether it is a good idea for Charles to experience the direct consequences of his behavior might go like this:

Ability

Since Charles has consistently been late to meetings, odds are he will repeat the behavior. But certainly, he can manage his schedule in a way that allows him to be prompt, especially since everyone else at the meeting has managed to that. So ability, at least in this case, is not an issue.

Impact on Charles

The impact on Charles will probably not severely curtail his willingness to make future decisions. After all, even though he may need to get better at time management, if he cannot even respond positively to this simple act, more difficult challenges might be too much for him. Because this is a minor offense, the upside will have more effect than the downside.

Impact on the Business

This is the most critical point. A manager must be aware of the impact of Charles missing vital information and weigh it against the productivity lost by starting meetings late.

I made sure my entire team was aware that all meetings were to start on time and anyone who is late will have to catch up. In my next meeting, we started on time and I signaled to the team my intention of making this work by closing the door to the meeting room and beginning. As expected, Charles was two minutes late, and I didn't break my stride to bring him up to speed. Charles asked if he missed anything, to which I replied in the positive but did not add anything to that statement. I reminded him that our meeting must progress so as not to waste other people's time. I did that matter-of-factly and without emotion.

After the meeting Charles came into my office to get caught up, but I made no special provisions to help him. I gave him my notes and asked that he return them when he was up to speed. If he needed more clarification I let him know that I could help him when it was convenient for me, not Charles.

At first this might seem a waste of time and unproductive; it was necessary, however. One of the greatest challenges a manager faces is letting an employee struggle with the negative consequences of his or her decisions. Because managers want people to succeed, they often try to minimize the direct impact of the consequences to the employee. When they do that, it may enable the behavior. This is indirectly harmful to the employee. The psychological definition of enabling is "a harmful form of helping." When managers prevent employees from experiencing the pain or pleasure of the consequences of their choices, they take away an opportunity for their employees to learn.

In this example of strategic nonintervention, Charles experiences the direct consequences of his actions. And he quickly learned how unproductive his behaviors were and adapted appropriately. I had faith in his ability to meet my expectations; he just needed a little guidance.

His previous manager's dependence on rewards and punishment to motivate Charles actually had the opposite effect. Managers so often create their own problems by reinforcing nonperformance and attempting to control him. They also contribute to Charles's nonperformance.

Henry Kissinger tells a story about an incident that happened when he was advising President Nixon. Kissinger and Nixon were in the Oval Office discussing Middle East negotiations, but could make no progress because Nixon's dog was chewing and barking at the rug. In frustration, Nixon reached into his desk and threw a bone to the dog. Upon seeing this, Kissinger said to Mr. Nixon, "Mr. President, you have just taught your dog to chew rugs."

By intervening and not letting Charles experience the direct consequences of his tardiness, his manager is teaching him to "chew rugs." Many managers teach their people to chew rugs when they don't allow them to experience the direct consequences of their decisions. They are trying to control the amount of discomfort an employee might feel.

Another example of this occurs when managers complain that they cannot get any work done because their people always come into their office to discuss problems. These managers might be reinforcing this behavior by volunteering the answer to the employees' problems.

One thing I always tell my people is that one of my expectations is for them to become good at their job without my help, for them to self-manage. This is, after all, my ultimate goal, to reduce my workload by developing my people. Managers who control take responsibility for problems that are not theirs and in which employees would benefit from making their own judgments. Managers who try to solve personality conflicts between employees are taking responsibility for problems outside of their control. A manager using strategic nonintervention would clarify the expectation that people are to respect each other's right to different opinions but find a way to resolve conflict without violence or yelling. Then let the employees work it out.

I once worked with a terrible manager in a medical device firm whose people were very much out of control: insubordinate, abusive, and downright nasty. When one of his people went off the rails screaming and making threats against another employee, I asked him how he could let this person continue to do this. To which he replied, "I don't know what his problem is. I've threatened to fire him a hundred times but it just never seems to have an impact."

Using the parenting analogy, when two kids are fighting and a parent steps in to try and stop the arguing, the children learn to come back to the parent to mediate any disputes. "Johnny said he won't be my friend if I don't do what he wants." A better suggestion is for the parent to say, "If you two want to continue to play together you will have to find a way to get along," and leave it at that. The kids will find a way to get along or suffer the consequences. The parent has clarified the expectation and used strategic nonintervention to let the children decide whether they want to experience the consequences or try to get along on their own. Because strategic nonintervention is strategic, a manager must make the critical judgment whether the individual employee is at an appropriate point on the responsibility continuum. If employees are not ready to hold themselves accountable and are not taking responsibility for their choices, a manager may have to communicate choices that the employee needs to make.

CHAPTER 5

The Facilitative Leaders' Last Resort

You are free to make whatever choice you want, but you are not free from the consequences of those choices.

–Stephen Covey

When a person continues to underperform even in the face of clear expectations, or his or her behavior becomes intolerable despite direct, honest, and constructive feedback, there is one more tool in a manager's set of management skills: the accountability conversation. Sometimes referred to as a "come to Jesus" meeting or being "called onto the carpet," an accountability discussion can be a helpful intervention when done correctly. But so often managers screw these discussions up, and for a couple of easily corrected mistakes.

Usually when a manager has an accountability discussion with an employee, it has one of two possible effects. The first and the best response from an employee is that he or she takes the conversation in the best light realizing that this is a serious issue. So, it is important that the manager approaches the situation with the same respect and honesty.

One issue that kept raising its head with Charles was his tendency to ignore our group decisions and undermine our efforts as a team. He did this by telling other departments that he didn't necessarily agree with our team's decisions. It was often brought to my attention by people from other departments that Charles did this on a regular basis. This was frustrating to me and my team as his behavior undercut the credibility of our decisions and the motivation of the group to include Charles in our discussions.

I had had several discussions about this with Charles in which he assured me that he was a changed man and totally focused on our efforts. Despite his, let's call them fabrications, I clearly communicated that it was not in his or anyone's best interest to sabotage our efforts. Despite my coaching, which became more and more directive, I continued to hear about his disagreements with our department from people within the organization. I decided that we had reached a point at which it was necessary to have a "come to Jesus" meeting with him.

Have a Plan

The first consideration a manager must make is, and which I had to consider with Charles's "back-stabbing" behavior, was whether this offense, issue, or subpar performance warrants an accountability discussion. A small infraction or mistake may not necessitate this sort of confrontation. Certainly, being late to a meeting is something that I believe can be addressed with some direct coaching and feedback. And unless it is extremely egregious or part of a larger, more ingrained set of behaviors, I certainly don't think that it is something a person should lose a job over.

Unfortunately, too many managers avoid confrontation by putting up with chronic behavior or moving a poorly performing employee to another part of the organization, like Charles. I jump on problems before they become issues. Sometimes direct and honest feedback can save an employee's career.

I had a salesperson who came into an offsite meeting wearing an inappropriate t-shirt with a sexist slogan on the front. I grabbed him before we started and told him to go back to his room and change it, even if he was late for the meeting. It wasn't the thing I would spend time asking him his reasons for donning this particular t-shirt. I simply stated that it was inappropriate and he needed to change it. Afterward, I had a conversation with him about his desired career path and explained that if this was the attitude he had toward women, it would certainly prevent me from putting him in a position where he had to oversee women's performance. He got the message because I was clear and unequivocal. This was not negotiable, and sometimes that is the position a manager must take. Especially if it is going to negatively impact others or the offenders' potential career path.

But getting back to a "come to Jesus" meeting discussion, if a manager has been responsible to an employee by communicating clear expectations, providing prompt feedback, and allowing the employee to learn and despite this, he or she continues to make bad choices, then the employee has chosen to live with the consequences.

The challenge a manager faces is to communicate the choice an employee needs to make from an impersonal, objective point of view. This is especially difficult because by the time it gets to this point in a business relationship, a manager is often frustrated with the employee. In this emotional atmosphere, he or she might take a controlling path and threaten punishment. There is a choice, however.

By communicating the logical choice an employee must make, a manager can get out of the way and not control. The employee is ultimately responsible for his or her life and can learn by being given an opportunity to make a choice. This is not a discussion that should be taken lightly.

A thoughtful plan, especially for an inexperienced manager, can help both sides get through the conversation reasonably well. It is crucial that the manager identifies what to say and how to say it. Preplanning helps to relieve some of the stress that naturally goes with this situation. Preplanning should include self-examination to identify whether the manager has provided expectations and feedback prior to communicating choices. I would first make sure you have your manager's support for this conversation especially if you will need his or her approval to follow through with the "incentive" to change. Because the last thing you want is for you to make an idle threat or consequences without the authority to follow through, it is important to clear that with HR or your manager at the very least.

Frame the Conversation

In this situation, your language should be more directive, than collaborative, but not unhelpful. Depending on how serious the issue is, you can adjust your tone to more serious and formal statement. Link the expectation and the negative behavior related to the expectation. The language should be firm and terse, and you must avoid getting derailed. You want to control this conversation. It is not a debate or a time to air other grievances.

You never want to have to revisit this issue, so being firm and clear is necessitated. And to some extent, it is not your responsibility, as a manager, to further coach and cajole. The end result of this discussion is to hand off the responsibility for the behavior to the employee; he or she is responsible whether they agree or not.

Communicating the seriousness of the issue is something that can be done well with how the conversation is framed. The phrase "I need to see you in my office" or "There is something we need to discuss that is relevant to your future in this company" sends a succinct message.

The Punishment Should Fit the Crime

This is where managers often find difficulty. While I use the term "punishment," what I mean is "consequences." But that said, the consequences can be seen by an employee as punishment, regardless of how well they are communicated. When it comes to connecting the consequence to the issue, it is necessary to make sure the person know that his or her problematic behavior has negative consequences for those who have to live with it.

First, remember that this is not about you; it is about running the business effectively, and this behavior is causing problems. Never threaten the employee that unless you see change, you will be the inflictor of the consequence. ("I'll see you never work in this town again!") When you think about it, this person is choosing to accept the consequences of his or her behavior by continuing the behavior and disregarding the impact his or her behavior is having on others and even himself, whether he or she knows it or not.

But the ultimate consequence, employment termination, is extreme and has a finality that is difficult to soft-pedal. And if, in fact, you do not have the backing of the company and HR, it may be an idle threat.

Some of the consequences, short of and different than losing a job, include a lower rating on the yearly performance review or the loss of a management career path or denial of working on desired projects. You should tie the consequence to the behavior whenever possible. A low rating on a performance review in the areas impacted by his or her behavior, connects the issue with the consequence. A limited career path is easily connected to working as a team or listening to other's input or helping others to achieve their goals. A manager should think it through so as to tie the consequence as logically as possible to the performance issue.

Coming back to Charles and his sabotaging behaviors, I began the discussion very directive. After one of my coworkers brought Charles's backstabbing behavior to my attention . . . again, I had to evaluate whether this person was trying to promote their own personal agenda or vendetta, but satisfied the feedback source was valid. Again, you must check, but not reveal your sources. I approached Charles with the intention of putting an end to this behavior once and for all.

"Charles, I need to see you in my office."

To which Charles replied, "I'm right in the middle of something. Can it wait?"

At this point, I wanted to send a clear message that this was an important and serious conversation we were about to have. "This matter is more important than anything you might be working on. We need to meet now."

That got his attention.

He followed me into my office and I intentionally shut the door behind us. That raised the tension, I hoped, and the stakes.

"Why did you want to see me boss?" Charles said.

"It has come to my attention that yet again you have undermined the effectiveness of the team by telling other departments that you disagree with some of the decisions we've made."

"Who told you that?"

This is where managers often get off track. The question is not legitimate if you've checked your sources.

"It doesn't matter. I've checked my sources and this is not the first time we've discussed this issue. So, I am confident in the source," I said holding my ground.

"Well, it matters to me."

"Regardless, I am not going to be drawn into a discussion of who said what especially because I know that this has happened."

This is where Charles made his first mistake, "Well, whoever said it is lying. I would never do something like that."

"Yes you have and yes you did, and now you've just lied to me. Would you like to continue?"

That stopped him. Charles looked like a deer in the headlights. I had him and he knew it. He also knew how serious this situation was; I was making it that way.

"Okay, I'm sorry. It won't happen again." His contrition was hopeful but this was a tactic he had tried before.

"Charles, you know that in meetings I solicit everyone's input including yours. We respectfully disagree while behind closed doors, but when we take a decision, I expect everyone to support it, even if they disagree with it. We have to present ourselves to other departments as a team."

Charles was despondent and let me go on.

"Your behavior is impacting the credibility of our group, credibility we need to ensure confidence in our decisions and direction. Do you understand that?"

"Um, yes." I was not so sure he bought into the idea, especially since his previous contrition was insincere.

"So you have to ensure this never happens again. We will not have this conversation again. If it happens again then it will seriously impact your yearly performance review and ultimately your income and ability to move up in the organization. I cannot recommend someone for a position of authority when he or she deliberately sabotages our efforts, regardless of how much you disagree with the decisions we take. That is not the behavior I or the company look at as a leadership quality."

He wasn't done yet with his challenge. "What are you saying here? I might lose my job over this?"

"No one is talking about losing a job, Charles. We are talking about a serious issue that needs to change, immediately."

"So my job is not in jeopardy, right?"

"Performance ratings are one measure of your effectiveness in your job. There are many others that play into a career direction. But understand, this is serious enough to impact your performance review. We can leave it at that."

I told Charles to sleep on it and we would discuss it further the next day. I wanted the message to sink in hoping that with a little time and reflection, he would get on board. In the end, I would find out whether Charles was on the bus or off the bus, regardless of what he told me. And I had decided that if it happened once more, we were done . . . and he would not see it coming. As I promised, we were not having another conversation on this topic.

Luckily for both of us, Charles did some deep soul-searching and came back the next day with a greatly revised attitude and approach. Perhaps his partner or friend gave him some good advice. I didn't know. But I was resolute and that is important. When you state the consequence, you must follow through. If you don't, you lose credibility above and below.

So, don't make promises you can't keep and use this type of discussion judiciously.

It quickly becomes obvious that communicating choices is a last resort for managers. Ensuring that clear expectations, feedback, and strategic nonintervention precede this step is the key to ensuring that this tactic is fair to the employee. It is critical that choices the employee must make are not related to what the manager wants. It isn't being "done" to the employee by the manager. Rather it is the choice the employee must make to live within the agreed-upon expectations of the company.

Accountability and the Facilitative Leader

Managers who try to make people responsible by holding them accountable fail to realize that this is a disguised attempt to make people conform. People do much better when they choose to take responsibility and hold themselves accountable.

Managers can take two different approaches to holding people accountable. The use of reward and punishment is seen by employees as an attempt to get them to "fall in line." Facilitating the process of taking responsibility allows the manager to get out of the way of an employee's learning. Strategic nonintervention allows the employee to learn by experiencing the direct consequences of his or her own behavior. Choice of consequences teaches by forcing employees to make decisions about their future behavior.

For managers to help people accept more responsibility, they need to have a more objective and impersonal perspective of their responsibilities. Managers are not responsible for their employees' behavior. They are responsible to them by providing expectations, feedback, and the opportunities to learn. Managers will have an easier time in the long run if they let their employees work out their own answers to problems.

The facilitative leader realizes people will take responsibility when they feel confident in the choices they make. People gain confidence by having opportunities to make choices and experience the direct consequences. Rewards and punishments are not direct consequences; they are the manager's consequences.

Helping people become responsible is about facilitating the opportunities for people to make choices and learn. It is realizing that people are works-in-progress and that experience is the best teacher. Watching people experience the negative consequences of their choices can be painful. It is pleasant when the consequences are positive. Facilitative leaders detach themselves and find pleasure in the learning that takes place from both types of choices. It can be painful to watch a person learn from bad decisions, but it results in people taking more responsibility for their lives and holding themselves accountable.

A manager's responsibility is to strategically allow people the opportunity to learn. When managers try to make people more responsible through reward and punishment, they are not managing. They are trying to control.

A manager's responsibility is to facilitate learning. There is a fine line between facilitating learning and abdicating responsibility. The difference is attention and involvement. Abdication is passive. Applying the concept of strategic nonintervention, using feedback and choice of consequences, is actively managing.

Charles's last problem stems from his manager's attempts to control his behavior through reward and punishment. Charles was deprived of his ability to learn. His manager tried to hold him accountable without allowing him to experience the consequences of his behavior.

In the end, Charles rose to the challenge. While not an overachiever, he became a productive and enthusiastic team member we all came to rely upon. He worked for me an additional year and a half at which time I recommended him for a promotion. When asked by his soon-to-be manager whether I had enough confidence in Charles's ability to meet the expectations of his new position, I quickly asked, "I think he can as long as you make clear to him the things that will be expected of him and his team."

And so, it goes . . .

Rewards and Punishment	Facilitating Responsibility
Demands compliance	Presents choices
Implies moral judgment	Objective and impersonal
Focuses on blame	Focuses on future
Uses positional power	Uses communication and persuasin

Can Facilitative Leadership Work in the American Business Culture?

Another way to pose the question in the title of this chapter is "Can a process-based management philosophy work in a results-based corporate culture?" The answer to this question can be found by examining a previous attempt to do exactly this.

The "Empowerment" Myth

In the late 1990s and early 2000s, management came to believe that decisions were best made by the people closest to the customer. This was the basis for the "empowerment" movement in corporations. Most companies subscribe to this "empowerment" as the best way to service customers.

In response to this belief, managers were encouraged to "empower" their people by giving them more authority to make decisions. In response, a manager's role shifted from control to ensuring that their people took responsibility and made smart decisions. When managers tried to "empower" their people, employees resisted being "empowered." As corporations and managers encountered unexpected difficulties, the movement slowed. Corporations, managers, and employees became disenchanted with the entire idea.

In frustration, managers frequently sought out consultants, corporate gurus, and motivational speakers to help them answer the questions, "How can we get people to make decisions and take responsibility?" and "How can we empower people?" Despite the time and money spent searching for the answers to these questions, it seems that even today the "empowerment" movement is still bogged down.

And the "empowerment" movement will continue to be bogged down until corporations realize that the true answer to the question "How can we empower people?" is "You can't." At least not with an autocratic-behaviorist management model.

When the "empowerment" philosophy was adopted into our "just do it" corporate culture, the result was a control-based approach to "empowering" people. Managers attempted to do this by giving people more responsibility and holding them accountable for making responsible decisions. The underlying misconception was that managers had the power to make people take responsibility.

As managers tried to give people responsibility, they were frustrated because people resisted taking it. They resisted because the methods used to "empower" people were thinly disguised attempts to control and manage results. They were attempts to externally motivate people to hold themselves accountable. In other words, management was trying to extrinsically motivate people to make an intrinsic decision to take responsibility.

True Empowerment

True empowerment occurs when an individual is given and accepts responsibility for a specific task or process by holding himself or herself accountable for the decisions regarding that task or process. Individuals are truly empowered when they make the intrinsic choice to take responsibility for consequences of their decisions.

But management continues to believe that people can be managed into taking responsibility. Management believes people will take responsibility even when they have little control over what is expected from them. When people are not given input into what they are going to be responsible for and held accountable to, why would they take responsibility?

People will take responsibility (or empower themselves) when they have some control over their environment and are confident in their abilities. Managers who attempt to "empower" people by giving them more responsibility and holding them accountable are simply trying to control them. The "empowerment" movement in the U.S. business culture was seen by employees for what it was: another attempt to manage results and not process.

Managers can help people empower themselves by helping them become responsible decision makers and giving them some control over what is expected from them. Managers can help people take more responsibility by concentrating more on process and less on results.

Which brings us back to this chapter's question, "Can a manager focus on the process of helping people become better decision makers in an environment that reinforces and rewards short-term results?" Put another way, "Can a manager focus on the long-term development of his or her people while still achieving short-term objectives?"

Management Focus Continuum

So far, this book has concerned itself with two different management approaches. It contrasted the autocratic-behaviorist approach of attempting to achieve results through control to the facilitative approach of building a solid foundation for people to become better decision makers. For purposes of illustration, this book depicted these as two different and separate management approaches. In fact, most managers play somewhere in between the two. Their behaviors fall somewhere along the management focus continuum.

Management Focus Continuum

Autocratic Behaviorist	Facilitative Leader
Control short-term behavior	Help people take responsibility
Focus on results	Focus on progress
Use rewards and punishment	Use fair and equitable accountability
See people as a set of behaviors	See people as works-in-progress

A manager's behavior will fall at different points along this continuum depending on three interdependent factors: the manager's own belief system, corporate pressure, and the amount of responsibility an employee is prepared to take.

Manager's Own Belief System

Managers who believe their job is to control short-term behavior to ensure results will use an autocratic-behaviorist approach to manage people.

When managers see themselves as being "in charge" of their people, they naturally use autocratic-behaviorist approaches. They will use accountability as the main tool to keep people in line.

Managers who believe their job is to help people become better decision makers will use a more facilitative management approach. Their behaviors will be further along the management focus continuum. The controlling manager is more likely to unilaterally define measurable expectations and hold people accountable. A manager whose focus is facilitating will collaboratively define and get agreement on standards and goals. The latter will set standards as boundaries; the former will set them as hard-and-fast rules. The autocratic-behaviorist approach utilizes results-based feedback in the form of praise and criticism, while the facilitative leader will use process-based encouragement.

A manager's belief system is one of the factors that influences at what point along the management focus continuum their behaviors fall. Another factor is corporate pressure.

Corporate Pressures

In the corporation of this still new century, there is incredible pressure on companies to achieve short-term bottom-line results. In the struggle to achieve short-term quarterly profit goals, U.S. corporations have downsized or "right-sized" to cut costs and increase productivity through technology and better utilization of resources, including human resources.

One of the ways in which companies have increased productivity is through longer work hours and harder work. It is common for workers to be expected to work longer hours with decreased or at least no relative increase in pay or benefits. Corporations are expecting more and more from employees and offering them less. Many workers believe corporations are expecting too much of them. Management expects people to work more and get less.

This ever-rising demand on employees' time and energy has resulted in unrealistic expectations. People will not hold themselves accountable or take responsibility for unrealistic expectations. They will refuse to be "empowered" in an environment in which they have no say over what and how much is expected of them.

Corporate pressure on managers to get more out of their people forces them to take a short-term controlling approach to get results. The ability of managers to help people become better decision makers runs directly counter to ever-rising demand for more productivity.

Ever-rising expectations can be satisfied only with ever-increasing resources. People's time and energy are limited resources. Management's attempt to "empower" people to take responsibility for unrealistic expectations runs counter to the definition of an "empowered" corporate culture.

This short-term focus drives true empowerment out of the corporation. A manager who wants to succeed in the eyes of the corporation must achieve results. In order to achieve results he or she must get people to perform to unrealistic expectations. When people don't agree to unrealistic expectations, the manager is left with the only management tool for this situation: control. In an attempt to manage to the end result, the manager defaults to accountability to get people to fall in line.

The result of this short-term focus is that managers feel they have little choice but to use an autocratic approach to managing. The "just do it" value system unfairly forces managers to adopt a control strategy. The more a company takes a short-term approach to business, the more managers will exhibit autocratic behaviors.

These three factors of belief system, corporate pressure, and employee ability all influence at what point a manager's behavior will fall along the management focus continuum. "Just do it" just doesn't.

At this point it might be easy for a manager to abdicate responsibility for adopting an autocratic-behaviorist approach to our results-driven culture. A manager might place the blame for using a controlling management style on the corporate bottom-line mentality. While there is ample evidence that corporate culture strongly influences the approach a manager takes, there is an element of personal choice as well.

A manager who makes the choice to begin the transition from an autocratic-behaviorist approach to that of a facilitative leader must start by examining his or her belief system. That is the first step for managers in taking responsibility for the part they play in their own management style.

To make the transition from an autocratic-behaviorist management approach to that of a facilitative leader, a manager will need to use a combination of results-based and process-based behaviors. Just as employees are making a transition from less responsible to more responsible, managers will need to make the transition from controlling short-term behavior to helping people become better decision makers. For this managers will need time, practice, and energy, plus a personal choice to look for longer-term improvement in employee behavior.

It is important to point out the critical role corporations play in this process. The drive toward unlimited growth and profits will eventually contribute to a workplace with expectations too high for employees to accept. Making people work in an environment in which they have little choice and ever-rising expectations will result in low employee morale. Morale does impact productivity.

Many workers feel that corporations are out of balance today. From the perspective of the employee, the most important corporate values in the 2000s are growth and profits. These values seem to supersede all others. Individual contribution, security, loyalty, and employee development become expendable when a company is in danger of missing its quarterly profit goals.

Management has come under increasing criticism for its inability to "walk its talk." Managers say the most important resource is the human resource, but they continue to put people below the bottom line. Management's behaviors don't support their words. The short-term profit goals always squeeze the long-term development of people. The long-term view is in short supply.

True leaders balance a short- and long-term view of their world. But putting a person at the head of a corporation doesn't make him or her a leader. Being in a position of authority may make a person a leader in his or her own eyes but not in the eyes of their people. The title of leader is earned not in things accomplished but in people developed. The more confidence people feel in themselves, the greater the leader.

This is the paradox: the person who wants to lead will never be a leader. To be a leader, a person must help others lead. To be a leader, a person must be willing to serve others. When a person is helping others to build confidence in themselves, he or she is leading.

Like the orchestra conductor, when a company has low morale, unhappy employees, and frustration with management, a facilitative leader will look first in the mirror to find solutions to these problems.

An autocratic behaviorist will look at the stock price.

Index

OTHER TITLES IN THE HUMAN RESOURCE MANAGEMENT AND ORGANIZATIONAL BEHAVIOR COLLECTION

- *The Illusion of Inclusion: Global Inclusion, Unconscious Bias, and the Bottom Line* by Helen Turnbull
- *On All Cylinders: The Entrepreneur's Handbook* by Ron Robinson
- *The Resilience Advantage: Stop Managing Stress and Find Your Resilience* by Richard S. Citrin and Alan Weiss
- *Successful Interviewing: A Talent-Focused Approach to Successful Recruitment and Selection* by Tony Miller
- *HR Analytics and Innovations in Workforce Planning* by Tony Miller
- *Success: Theory and Practice* by Michael Edmondson
- *Leading The Positive Organization: Actions, Tools, and Processes* by Thomas N. Duening, Donald G. Gardner, Dustin Bluhm, Andrew J. Czaplewski, and Thomas Martin Key
- *Performance Leadership* by Karen Moustafa Leonard and Fatma Pakdil
- *The New Leader: Harnessing The Power of Creativity to Produce Change* by Renee Kosiarek
- *Employee LEAPS: Leveraging Engagement by Applying Positive Strategies* by Kevin E. Phillips
- *Feet to the Fire: How to Exemplify and Create the Accountability That Creates Great Companies* by Lorraine A. Moore
- *Deconstructing Management Maxims* by Kevin Wayne
- *The Real Me: Find and Express Your Authentic Self* by Mark Eyre
- *Life of a Lifetime: Inspiration for Creating Your Extraordinary Life* by Christoph Spiessens

Announcing the Business Expert Press Digital Library

Concise e-books business students need for classroom and research

This book can also be purchased in an e-book collection by your library as

- *a one-time purchase,*
- *that is owned forever,*
- *allows for simultaneous readers,*
- *has no restrictions on printing, and*
- *can be downloaded as PDFs from within the library community.*

Our digital library collections are a great solution to beat the rising cost of textbooks. E-books can be loaded into their course management systems or onto students' e-book readers. The **Business Expert Press** digital libraries are very affordable, with no obligation to buy in future years. For more information, please visit **www.businessexpertpress.com/librarians**. To set up a trial in the United States, please email **sales@businessexpertpress.com**.

www.ingramcontent.com/pod-product-compliance
Lightning Source LLC
Chambersburg PA
CBHW062042200326
41519CB00017B/5110